RATIONALITY, NATIONALISM AND POST-COMMUNIST MARKET TRANSFORMATIONS

To my parents

Rationality, Nationalism and post-Communist Market Transformations

A comparative analysis of Belarus, Poland and the Baltic States

ANDREW SAVCHENKO
Thomas J. Watson Jr. Institute for International Studies
Brown University

Routledge
Taylor & Francis Group

LONDON AND NEW YORK

First published 2000 by Ashgate Publishing

Reissued 2018 by Routledge
2 Park Square, Milton Park, Abingdon, Oxon OX14 4RN
711 Third Avenue, New York, NY 10017, USA

Routledge is an imprint of the Taylor & Francis Group, an informa business

Notice:
Product or corporate names may be trademarks or registered trademarks, and are used only for identification and explanation without intent to infringe.

Publisher's Note
The publisher has gone to great lengths to ensure the quality of this reprint but points out that some imperfections in the original copies may be apparent.

Disclaimer
The publisher has made every effort to trace copyright holders and welcomes correspondence from those they have been unable to contact.

A Library of Congress record exists under LC control number: 99085929

ISBN 13: 978-1-138-70168-7 (hbk)
ISBN 13: 978-1-138-70166-3 (pbk)
ISBN 13: 978-1-315-20395-9 (ebk)

Contents

Acknowledgements

I thank Jens Kaalhauge Nielsen whose deep commitment to social theory and unrelenting optimism he brought to our numerous long conversations kept stimulating my interest in relations between economy and society and thus helped to lay theoretical foundation for this book.

During my field work in Belarus, Pavel Daneiko from the Institute of Privatization and Management in Minsk and Vladimir Usoski, currently with the Belarusian Academy of Sciences, kindly shared with me their knowledge of Belarusian economy and provided valuable insights into its *modus operandi*.

This book is based on my doctoral dissertation which would not have been possible without intellectual help given to me freely and generously by my mentors. Members of my dissertation committee guided me through all stages of my graduate program. Professor Dietrich Rueschemeyer, Chair of the committee, helped me to develop the ideas of this research and provided critical yet encouraging comments. Professor Abbott Gleason kept alive my interest in history and ensured that it remained an important facet of my study. I am grateful to Professor Robert Marsh for his assistance with the methodological and empirical aspects of my research. At the earlier stage of my work, numerous fruitful conversations with Professor Martin U. Martel, who was a member of my dissertation committee until his death in December of 1995, were crucial in my intellectual development and understanding of the richness and complexity of sociological theory. I am fortunate to have these scholars as my mentors and would like to express my deep gratitude to them.

Financial support provided by the Department of Sociology and the Watson Institute for International Studies at Brown, together with a dissertation fellowship from the Institute for the Study of World Politics, was indispensable for the completion of my research and is gratefully acknowledged.

Introduction

In 1989-91, when the Soviet-dominated system was crumbling rapidly throughout Eastern Europe and in the Soviet Union, most Western observers hailed these developments as an unconditional triumph of the free market and a free society. The key word in the discourse immediately following the collapse of the Soviet system was "free". This is not surprising since a dichotomous vision of the world was firmly entrenched in both Western and Soviet camps. Therefore, the collapse of the "unfree" society was perceived as an immediate precursor to "freedom": social freedom in the shape of civil society; political freedom through representative democracy; and economic freedom through the market. Although the euphoria soon subsided, it contributed to the emergence of an optimistic, individualistic and instrumentalist paradigm of post-Communist transition. The paradigm was optimistic because it envisioned substantial improvement in all spheres of social, political, and economic life in a very short period of time. It was individualistic because it regarded the unfettered energy and elan of individual actors as the sole driving force of transition. It was instrumentalist because it was concerned almost exclusively with means rather than ends; it stated what ought to be done to promote the envisioned reforms but it paid much less attention to the real world actors and their actual preferences. This paradigm was not totally divorced from reality. It did present a partially correct image of the post-Communist state of affairs and, in some cases, provided an approximate blueprint for social, political, and economic reforms. However, it did not explain some important phenomena, particularly, the differences in shape and pace of transition between different countries. It regarded the developments in the former Soviet-type societies as a transition from some known point of departure to an equally well known outcome. In so doing, it discounted the possibility of more complex transformation to something as yet unknown or a long stagnation and subsequent degeneration to something known but not desirable (such as a Third World economy and society).

In this book I attempt to make a comparative analysis of market transition as an important element of the post-Soviet transformation process. Many studies have shown that the market itself, even though it may be free from arbitrary interference by the state, is by no means free from the influence of the supporting institutions. I intend to demonstrate that the transition from the

1

essentially non-market to the essentially market economic system is a considerably less free and rational process than the operation of a developed capitalist market. It is conditioned by the pre-existing pattern of traditions, values and institutions not necessarily directly connected with the economic system. The real progress of market reforms is not necessarily based on rational calculations free from non-economic considerations. Rather, at each stage economic reforms are influenced by the existing value system which to a large extent determines their success or failure. Instead of being a rational process of transition from a less efficient to a more efficient economic system, market reforms are a complex concatenation of events with not always predictable or even anticipated outcomes.

Now, almost ten years after the political and economic collapse of the Soviet Union and its satellite states in Eastern Europe, cross-national variations of shape, pace and direction of socio-economic transitions in the post-Soviet world have become apparent. Some important explanations of these differences in early transitions have already been presented. The "Path Dependency" theory (Stark, 1994) maintains that particular economic features that developed in the Communist past are shaping the process of transition to a capitalist market economy and that this must be taken into account when assessing progress to date or making future projections. Although Stark concentrates on the analysis of four East European countries (Poland, Hungary, Czechoslovakia, East Germany), his approach provides important insights into the more general nature of path dependency. In this book I examine whether the phenomenon of path dependency is confined exclusively to economic institutions and whether it affects not only the shape, but also the speed and (more importantly) direction of post-Soviet transformations.

This inquiry employs a comparative historical approach introduced and developed by Arend Lijphart (1971) and Theda Skocpol (1979; Skocpol and Somers, 1980) and successfully applied to the analysis of post-Soviet social developments by David Laitin (1995). My comparison mainly focuses on transitional processes in four former Soviet republics: Belarus, Lithuania, Latvia, and Estonia. They are examined against the comparative background of Poland. The latter is included in this study because it experienced the most ambitious attempt of a deliberately conducted rapid market transformation based upon the theoretical premises of neoclassical economics. Thus, even a brief analysis of the Polish model of reforms contributes to the test of validity of the paradigm of socio-economic transition mentioned above.

All countries included in this analysis had similar economic institutions structure prior to the Soviet collapse. They are located in the same region, suffer from similarly scarce supply of natural resources and are endowed with a similarly skilled workforce. They were roughly equally dependent on Russia for their supply of energy and important raw materials. In short, as late as 1990 they used to have a basic overall comparability in economic structure and institutions. However, their developments after independence are already markedly different.

Poland and the three Baltic states are steadily moving toward a modern capitalist market economy (even though they do not follow the path of transition anticipated by local reformers and Western observers) and seek inclusion in the West European economic system. By contrast, Belarus is lagging behind in its market reforms and seeks to retain economic and political ties with Russia. The differences are so profound that they cannot be regarded merely as matters of degree or idiosyncratic peculiarities of various economic reforms. One of the main tasks of this book is to investigate causes of these differences. In this analysis I proceed from an assumption that some features of old regimes in the countries included in this analysis contributed to variations in their post-Soviet transformations.

The study concentrates on the time period between 1989 and 1994. Belarus, Poland, and the Baltic states were roughly equally distant from the developed capitalist market economy as late as 1989-90. However, by 1994 it had become apparent that market development in Poland and the three Baltic states has gained momentum and become irreversible. At the same time, in Belarus market transformations were going slowly and in the summer of 1994 the policy of market reforms had been abandoned by the new Byelorussian government whose policies today include deliberate avoidance of market transformation and the preservation of Soviet-type economic structures. Another unusual aspect that makes Belarus stand apart from most newly independent states is almost complete absence of nationalist self-assertiveness of its policies. Indeed, the opposite is the case: Belarus's foreign policy is increasingly directed toward closer integration with Russia. Unlike the neighboring Baltic states and Poland, where national sentiment strongly influences policy formation, Belarus is willing to surrender important elements of its national sovereignty. The combination of these two phenomena -- the lack of nationalism and the abandonment of economic reforms -- is too salient to be ignored.

Using Belarus as an important counterpoint in the comparative analysis of socio-economic changes in Eastern Europe allows me to formulate a tentative hypothesis: The emergence and development of nationalism in post-

Communist European countries is among the factors that have a positive impact on the development of the modern market economy.

The focus of my inquiry is on the particular moment of transition from the essentially non-market to the essentially market economy (or, as in Byelorussian case, the lack of such a transition). The main question in this context is whether the market developments in the late Soviet and post-Soviet societies were an autonomously originated and self-supporting process introduced by the reformist politicians whose primary concern was to improve economic performance or were influenced by factors extraneous to the economic system.

In this book I will demonstrate that the emergence of market economies in late Soviet and post-Soviet societies was only one element of a larger process of socio-economic and political transformations that can be presented as the following chain of events:

The paramount goal of the opposition leaders who came to power in Poland and the Baltics after the collapse of Soviet domination was full national independence. Their dissatisfaction with the centrally planned economy was caused not only by its low performance but also because it was directed from Moscow rather than respective national capitals and thus was seen as a vehicle of imperial domination. The desired secession from the Soviet sphere of influence posed the question of economic survival. The new rulers seemed to have only a limited choice of economic options: either to retain centrally controlled, essentially non-market economic system, or to introduce market reforms. This set of choices emerged in the context of intellectual discourse about comparative advantages of market versus non-market economies.

The discourse, well presented in scholarly and professional journals, started well before the collapse of the Communist regime. Very soon the discussion became rather one-sided, pro-market orientations rapidly gaining ground and crowding out alternative points of view. It concentrated on a particular vision of the market, the one based on abstract neoclassical models. In this vision the laissez-faire market was endowed with exclusively positive features, such as high efficiency and the potential for rapid economic growth. At the same time, a suggestion of even a moderate state intervention in the economy was presented as a vestige of the old-style, socialist economic thinking. Any possibility of a third way, e.g. an essentially market system where the state would remain among major economic actors, was discounted even as a temporary measure. The transition to the market was viewed as a rapid process whereby the macroeconomic stabilization is accompanied by swift changes in the property rights system, divestment of the state of all its assets and the emergence of private economic agents in place of the formerly state-owned enterprises. The transition was expected to be completed in a matter of months.

Many of the post-Communist rulers, former leaders of nationalist and other opposition movements and parties, belonged to intellectual elites and were responsive to that discourse. At the time when even the economists have inordinately positive expectations of the market as both the end and means of economic reforms, former opposition leaders, most of whom were not trained in economics, tended to become uncritical about the hypothetical advantages of the market and the possibilities of its rapid implantation into the existing economic system. They perceived the market as a logical and easy choice of economic system for an independent state since it seemed to provide solutions to the problems created by economic separation from the empire. What they envisioned was not a gradual emergence and strengthening of market economy but rather a full-fledged market introduced by a government decree.

Market reforms did not produce the expected results in part because of opposition from the groups with vested interests in the old economic system. This is particularly true for the privatization of large state enterprises, whose employees enjoy significant political clout. However, in those countries where reforms are conducted consistently, some of their elements (in particular, economic liberalization and small-scale privatization) gave rise to market forces and created new social groups which have a stake in development of the market economy. These positive results of market reforms are not the ones anticipated by the reformers. However, they set the market mechanism in motion and thus represented a real success of the first stage of economic reforms.

The above description, albeit schematic, of the market transformations and the accompanying events in post-Soviet societies differs from the early accounts of these events presented by many proponents of the market who were eager to get rid of the inefficient Soviet-type economy in what proved to be an impossibly short time. In their interpretation, after the collapse of the Communist regime the new political leaders understand that they have to make a "stark and rational choice" in favor of the immediate and all-embracing transition to "*extremely liberal* economy in a *radical* deregulation" (Aslund, 1992, p. 22; italics added). The choice is rational because it is based on a well-developed theory of transition in which the available knowledge about the starting point, the goal, and the means to achieve it is equally reliable and well detailed. In this research I intend to test the validity of this account by contrasting it with the actual state of knowledge about market economy and market reforms in the late Communist and early post-Communist societies.

The book includes a brief discussion of market models. Neoclassical economics perceives the market as a universal system and only tacitly assumes that supporting societal institutions are "out there". In my research the emphasis is on institutional change and therefore the neoclassical market paradigm is less useful. I partly follow the general discussion of markets provided by Polanyi (1944) and recently elaborated (e.g., by Swedberg (1994) and Portes (1994)). These authors emphasize that different types of markets are embedded in and maintained by corresponding societal structures. An institutional approach to markets leads to an important corollary regarding transitional economies. The transition from a non-capitalist to a capitalist system of exchange and allocation of scarce resources is a combination of the spontaneous activities of individual actors and deliberate state actions. The former create exchange networks which, if left alone, do not necessarily lead to the development of modern capitalist markets. The latter shape the incipient market into a particular model by institution-building. In this book I will discuss how particular combinations of these factors lead to variations of transition processes across the countries included in this analysis.

Clearly, in order for market reforms to be successful they must be legitimated. Legitimation is especially important since facilitating market development may contradict the interests of powerful and politically important groups. Therefore, the source of legitimation should be consonant with strong values shared by an effective plurality of the population. It seems that anticipation of increased economic efficiency cannot be the primary motive for market reforms, since structural changes, while leading to gains in efficiency in the long run, initially entail drastic, and often painful, economic and social dislocations. Therefore, a way of ensuring the legitimation of market reforms lies outside the economic realm.

In many East European countries of the early post-Soviet period the most salient feature of the value-system was nationalism combined with the rejection of the Communist ideology. It is not surprising that in the Baltic states legitimation of market reforms took on nationalist overtones, while in Poland laissez-faire capitalism was presented as the only means to break with the Communist past. Economic policies of the three Baltic states have been designed to distance their economies from Russia, despite the fact that continuing that association would make economic transformation less painful. In Poland, the reformers' actions have been shaped by their vision of a particular model of the social and economic system. Some Polish scholars suggest that this vision includes not only abstract economic models, but a profound nationalist element, a synthesis of Western economic theories and Polish national mythology, and a desire for the inclusion of Poland in the European community of nations (e.g. Burszta, 1995).

It appears that in the process of social change, the existing value-patterns influence the institutional transformation and that supporting institutions are essential for the emergence of a market economy. Parsons' idea that social change and differentiation proceed along a diagonal of pattern-maintenance -- goal attainment in the four-function paradigm (Parsons, 1977, p. 288) seems to fit the pattern of socio-economic transformation in the post-Soviet world. The importance of social values in the rapid political and economic change has been pointed out by Chalmers Johnson (1982) and Samuel Huntington (1968). This suggests that the "Values -- Legitimation -- Socio-Economic Transformations" axis should be central for this book.

The study will include an analysis of the issues relating to legitimation and support. Theoretical approaches to the concept of legitimation have undergone major changes since their introduction by Max Weber. Parsons pointed out important connections between legitimation, political action, and power, emphasizing that legitimation increases political power (Parsons, 1960, p. 281; Parsons, 1969, p. 345). Later, Habermas has explicitly related legitimacy to the performance of economic and political subsystems of society (Habermas, 1976, p. 36). Links between power and legitimation are also discussed by Stinchcombe, who attempts to equate legitimacy with an ability to call upon centers of power for support (Stinchcombe, 1968, p. 162). Although legitimacy cannot be simply reduced to sheer power, Stinchcombe's approach provides insights into the differentiation of legitimacy within social structure. Eisenstadt emphasized importance for legitimation of support by organized elite groups rather than by the masses (Eisenstadt, 1963, p. 198). This idea is further elaborated by Rueschemeyer, who distinguishes between legitimacy emerging among the population in general and legitimacy within the apparatus of domination (Rueschemeyer, 1986, p. 67). Bunce (1992, p. 29) pointed out the importance of changing legitimation patterns among the ruling elites for the socio-economic transformations in the late Soviet and post-Soviet societies. Staniszkis (1992, pp.187-188) maintains that nationalistic feelings served as an important element of the intra-elite legitimation pattern as well as the legitimation of the local elites among their constituencies in post-Soviet states.

It is important to ask what kind of legitimation was used within the ruling elites, between their particular groups and strata. The specific focus of this discussion is on the legitimation of a new economic system, as this legitimation pattern emerges in a dialogue between the aspiring new rulers and the experts.

In the study of legitimation patterns I use the information collected during interviews with government officials and political figures in Belarus. Byelorussian, Lithuanian, and Latvian newspapers and other periodicals represent another important source of information. Macroeconomic information was collected from publications by national statistical offices, international economic agencies, and secondary literature. Information regarding policy decisions was obtained by means of interviews, analysis of internal documents of government agencies, and secondary sources.

Problems with economic data relating to post-Communist transformations are discussed in detail in Chapter One. At this point I would like to emphasize that those problems proved to be numerous and complex, thus forcing me to rely heavily on secondary sources.

The book begins with a discussion of theories of transformation and social change. World System Theory, the Marxist theory of social change, and the neoclassical economic model of transition will be contrasted with an essentially Weberian approach to social transformations.

My research is primarily concerned with the influence of the emerging value-systems (particularly their nationalist element) and changing distribution of power in post-Soviet societies on the market transition. The book includes four chapters. In Chapter One, I discuss alternative approaches to social changes and market development, particularly stressing two contrasting paradigms: the one that regards social change as being driven primarily by structural transformations, and another that recognizes the importance of changes in value-systems. After discussing these two paradigms, we assess their suitability for an analysis of post-Soviet transitions. The chapter also includes a brief comparison of structural and cultural features of Belarus and the Baltic states against the comparative background of Poland. The main purpose of this chapter is to find whether the structural differences account for the entire spectrum of variations in post-Soviet developments.

Chapter Two deals with various models of the market and their perceptions in late Soviet and post-Soviet societies. I examine the attitude toward the market among the intellectuals, political leaders, and the opposition. The place of market reforms in programs of nationalist movements and parties will be identified. In this chapter I examine the issues relating to the role of expert economic knowledge in the process of economic transformation. Since in Soviet societies expert knowledge of market economies and market transition was scarce, experts provided broad perceptions of the desirable economic system rather than detailed and clear-cut models of transition. Comparison of market perceptions in different countries will be used to establish variations among them. It is possible that differences in the attitudes toward and perceptions of market economy can account for variations in market transitions.

In Chapter Three, I discuss social and economic factors shaping the first stages of policy decisions relating to market reforms in the post-Soviet states. Opposition mass movements and parties in post-Soviet societies, their bases of popular support and the spread of nationalist sentiments among various social groups will be analyzed. The economic impact of changing relations with Russia as the former imperial power as well as other economic realignments will be examined.

Chapter Four examines the actual implementation of market reforms in post-Soviet countries. Both the intentions of reformers and unintended consequences of reforms will be discussed. Alternative strategies of market reforms (in particular, mass privatization vs. liberalization) and their results will be compared. In this chapter I examine the role of small private enterprises that either were privately owned when founded or emerged as a result of small-scale privatization. Their role in market development will be compared to that of large formerly state-owned enterprises which were subject to mass privatization programs. The principal factors determining success or failure of market transitions will be examined. The chapter also includes an analysis of property rights theory as a theoretical foundation of market reform policies in post-Communist countries. Property rights theory asserts that economic efficiency depends on a particular structure of property rights. It explains suboptimal performance of economic systems by the persistence of an outmoded structure of property rights that is maintained by the power of the state. A particular interpretation of this approach became the main theoretical frame of reference for reform policies in post-Communist societies of Eastern Europe and the former Soviet Union. According to this interpretation, rapid changes of the property rights system, particularly the mass-scale privatization of large industrial enterprises, result in immediate improvement of economic performance. On the other hand, proponents of a gradual transformation of Soviet-type economies insist that the market progress is represented mostly by gradual development of small private enterprises, while the large-scale privatization is fraught with political controversy and in most cases is less successful. In Chapter Four I attempt to to test these contrasting points of view by analyzing post-Soviet economic transformations in Poland, the three Baltic states and Belarus in the years of 1991-94.

I conclude the book with the final comments on the nature of the post-Communist transformation process and assess the usefulness of the theories that claim the explanatory and predictive power regarding this transformation.

1 Theoretical Approaches to Economic Transformation: A Comparison

Post-Soviet socio-political and economic transformations present a challenge for theories of modernization and development, as well as more general theoretical paradigms of social change. It seems that there is no coherent and sufficiently detailed body of thought that can explain the variegated patterns of these transformations whose scope and significance match those of the most drastic social changes in this century. The main developmental theories are almost absent from the discourse on the causes of recent post-Soviet transformations. At the same time, the aftermath of the Soviet system is marked by the emergence and proliferation of ad hoc approaches to problems of transformation that combine weak theoretical foundations and strong prescriptive elements. These approaches usually originate among the outside observers and consultants from various international agencies, such as the IMF and the World Bank. In the theoretical vacuum and economic disarray of post-Soviet countries they are often accepted and used for formulation of reform policies. Results of such experiments more often than not are disappointing and damaging for the overall transition progress. However, before their inadequacy becomes evident, they contribute to the formation of a particular image of post-Soviet transformations, both in the West and in post-Soviet countries.

In this book we discuss differences in market transitions that started to take place in Eastern Europe in the early nineties. How would the existing theories (and "practical" ad hoc approaches[1]) explain these differences? The economic system occupies a central place in most theories of socio-economic transformation. However, as we shall see from the discussion that follows, many of them tend to treat economic processes as independent variables. In our case, the question is about the departure from one economic system and the emergence of another one. Is this process driven predominantly by economic factors? The answer to this question will to a large extent determine the relevance of the existing theories of socio-economic transformation for our inquiry.

Intellectual Traditions Explaining Social Transformation

There are three major intellectual traditions that attempt to establish general characteristics of socio-economic transformations as well as their causes and outcomes: Marxist, Utilitarian-Positivist, and Weberian. These traditions are relevant for our inquiry because they influence more recent and specific theories concerned with transformation processes. Therefore, they deserve a brief discussion.

The Marxist tradition, originating in works of Karl Marx and Friedrich Engels, seeks to explain socio-economic transformations in a determinist, materialist, universalist, and conflictual way. According to this tradition, all social processes are determined by the material factors, namely, production forces.

"In the social production of their life, men enter into definite relations that are indispensable and independent of their will, relations of production which correspond to a definite stage of development of their material productive forces" (quoted in Lichtheim, 1961). This famous statement, which Marx made in the preface to *A Contribution to the Critique of Political Economy*, still reflects a core element of any theory which claims affiliation with Marxism. Despite various interpretations of the original Marxism by later theorists, the predominance of material, economic factors in all social processes remains unquestionable.

Changes in production forces gradually accumulate until they come in contradiction with the existing relations of production. Then a structural change occurs, rapidly and often violently, driven by conflict between classes. In the orthodox Marxist vision of social development each society has to pass through several stages (primitive society, slave-owning, feudal, capitalist) and to reach the final stage: communist classless society where contradictions and conflicts no longer exist. The Marxist tradition acquired its basic shape in works of its founding fathers and then continued to develop, adjusting to changing socio-economic conditions, without any significant breach in continuity. It is still identifiable today, with a plethora of scholars explicitly stating their affinity with Marxism and building their theoretical schemes on the basic premises of this tradition.[2]

The case of the Soviet-type societies, where property relations were hardly distinguishable as a basis for political and economic power, presented a challenge to the proponents of the above approach. However, some scholars tried to circumvent an apparently insurmountable problem and fit these societies into an essentially Marxist theoretical scheme. Following Milovan Djilas' definition of the power-holders in the Communist social system as a "new class", Marxian scholars in the West attempted to elaborate on it and include it in the class approach to the analysis of the Soviet-type societies. Among the most notable defenders of a Marxist approach to the issue of social stratification and power in Communist countries are Michael Burawoy, Tom Bottomore, as well as George Konrad and Ivan Szelenyi. The main argument of these authors is that since the Party-dominated state apparatus exercised control over the economy, the position of its members was essentially similar to that of the propertied class.[3]

The view of the Soviet governing minority as a latent capitalist class deriving its power in political decision-making from the property ownership disguised as a state control over the economy has a certain logical appeal. However, there are some inconsistencies in this view which should be discussed. Equating control by the state apparatus over the economy with relations of property is not entirely persuasive. This control is exercised collectively by an organization with a multi-level and multi-divisional structure where responsibilities and benefits of individual members associated with property relations are completely obscured. We can only speak of one collective owner of all economic assets in the whole country. At the same time, the concept of a propertied class implies individual owners with clearly distinguishable rights, responsibilities, and benefits entailed by their institutionalized position of ownership. There are some other contradictions which make the class approach to the Soviet system less than useful. On the other hand, the notion of ruling elites does not produce this confusion. This is recognized by Bottomore when he states that there is a visible distinction between elites and ruling class and that the political system as it existed in the Communist countries approached the pure type of "power elites".[4] This statement contradicts his position on the issue expressed in the same book and quoted above. This contradiction itself indicates the difficulty even for a devoted Marxist to apply a Marxian scheme to the Communist societies. Scholars in the field of Soviet studies who were more concerned with a correct description of the Soviet society rather than the preservation of a particular theoretical system often hesitated to apply the class approach to the Soviet rulers.[5]

The Utilitarian-Positivist tradition does not represent as coherent and consistent a body of thought as the Marxian tradition. However, it is distinguishable from other broad approaches to socio-economic transformation. Its origins can be traced back to the works of Auguste Comte and Herbert Spencer. Both authors saw society as a system that develops through stages. Unlike Marxists, they did not emphasize material conditions and class conflict as the main driving forces of this development. Instead, they perceived ideas (Comte) and combined processes of growth, structural differentiation and integration (Spencer) as the main determinants of socio-economic transformation. The positivist component of this tradition can be traced back to Auguste Comte. He regarded the highest stage of social development, industrial society, as positivistic, that is, governed according to ideas that are derived from empirical observations and developed according to the principles of positive science. Decisions made on the basis of such ideas have predictable outcomes. Spencer can be credited with the elaboration of the utilitarian component of this tradition. He envisioned modern industrial society as being free from state controls, where increased productivity is the main goal which is to be achieved by unfettered pursuit of individual gain.[6]

When in 1937 Talcott Parsons noted in the introduction to *The Structure of Social Action* that nobody reads Spencer, the statement correctly reflected the contemporary attitude among sociologists. It was much less true for economists who, regardless of whether they actually read Spencer (or Comte), based their theories on utilitarian and positivist assumptions. The "Keynesian revolution" did not eliminate the essentially utilitarian-positivist character of economics. Keynes himself emphasized the intellectual affiliation of his theory with ideas of Jeremy Bentham, a founding father of utilitarianism (Keynes, 1936 (1964), pp. 352-353). Keynes introduced the state as an actor in economic process, but state actions were seen as based on empirically verifiable information and leading to predictable outcomes. Recent changes in economic theory (in particular, the emergence of Economics of Property Rights) did not change its close affinity with the Utilitarian-Positivist tradition.[7]

The increased influence of the Utilitarian tradition on sociology started in the late sixties. Not surprisingly, it came from economics, some of its exponents being economists attempting to expand their vision of social system into the domain of sociology. Gary Becker, James Coleman, Mancur Olson were among the most forceful advocates of a rational utilitarian approach to all social processes. According to them, these processes can be reduced to actions of individuals based on rational calculations of potential gains and losses. Individuals act according to their rationally perceived self-interest unless their actions are forcibly restricted (by the state or some other authority).

A different direction of approach to social change is represented by the Weberian tradition, which is more flexible and inclusive. While it does not ignore the influence of structural elements, it recognizes a role of values and ideas as a crucial component of socio-economic transformation. This paradigm emphasizes the significance of cultural elements in changes of economic structures and the importance of legitimation in maintaining and transformation of social system. Raymond Aron wrote that Weber's vision of social transformation as expressed in *The Protestant Ethic and the Spirit of Capitalism* is a "refutation of historical materialism" (Aron, 1965, vol. 2, p.296). Weber, as Marx, sought to identify the origins of capitalism and its internal logic of development, but the only thing these two scholars had in common was the subject of their inquiries. Almost every element of Weber's theory is the opposite of its Marxist counterpart. In tacit opposition to the materialist, determinist and totalist theoretical construction created by Marx, Weber asserts that sometimes values and ideas can influence change of economic system, social transformation is a matter of probability rather than some predetermined pattern, and each society is unique at each particular stage of its existence.

Weber's works stand in opposition to the Utilitarian-Positivist tradition. The introduction of two types of rationality (instrumental and value-rationality) as well as the classification of types of action where instrumental-rational type was only one of four (the other three being value-rational, emotional-affective, and traditional) constituted major arguments against the utilitarian vision of social action as based on calculable self-interest. At the same time, Weber's insistence on the importance of intuitive understanding for social science rejected positivist claims that empirically verifiable information is the sole source of social knowledge. Weber's view of social change as a concatenation of historical events with often unforeseeable outcomes sharply contradicted the positivist vision of social transformation as a universal and predictable process.

The Weberian paradigm was later theoretically developed and elaborated. Talcott Parsons, when he started to build his theory of social action, reinforced Weber's rejection of the Utilitarian-Positivist approach to society.[8] He noted that in the utilitarian frame of reference "from the point of view of the actor, scientifically verifiable knowledge of the situation in which he acts becomes the only significant orienting medium. *Given the assumption that there is no alternative selective standard in the choice either of means or ends, action becomes essentially involuntary.*" (Parsons 1937 (1968), pp. 61, 66, italics added). Parsons' polemics with utilitarians was directed against the frame of reference common for contemporary economics. For Parsons the existence of a particular social order was a necessary precondition for the market economy.[9] He continued this polemics in the later period of his work arguing that even though principles of economics as a discipline may be based on the assumption of rational individual action, they are not the same as elementary principles of social behavior (Alexander, 1983, p.117).

In *Economy and Society*, which he wrote together with Neil Smelser, Parsons paid special attention to mechanisms of socio-economic change. He maintained that changes in economic structure are not necessarily initiated by purely economic phenomena. Parsons' treatment of economy as a sub-system of a larger social system opened the door for sociological analysis of economic processes.[10] Later, these ideas have found the most abstract theoretical reflection in the AGIL model and the notion of cybernetic hierarchy.

An essentially Weberian view on interrelations between social and economic processes was expressed by Juergen Habermas with particular application to the process of change in modern society (Habermas, 1975). Habermas perceived the social system as consisting of four interrelated subsystems: the economic system, the administrative system, the legitimation system, and the socio-cultural system. He specifically deals with crisis tendencies, but the main postulates of his theory are applicable to the issue of social change in general (crisis being a particular case of social change). Habermas' emphasis on the involvement of the state (administrative system) in the functioning of the modern economic system combined with the inability of the administrative system to generate a requisite quantity of rational decisions contributes to the theoretical foundations of the study of non-economic phenomena influencing economic structural change. His view of the socio-cultural system as a locus of motives for social action places values among the factors influencing socio-economic transformation.

A brief outline of intellectual traditions in approach to socio-economic change makes it possible to trace two main paradigms of such an approach. The first paradigm analyses social change along the axis "material structural change -- conflict of interest groups -- institutional transformation". The axis presented in the second paradigm is "changing value-system and ideas -- changes in legitimation pattern -- institutional transformation". The first paradigm combines the Marxist and Utilitarian-Positivist traditions. The second paradigm is represented by the Weberian tradition and its later development. In the following sections of this chapter we will discuss specific theories of socio-economic transformation and development and trace the influence of these traditions on them.

Theories of Socio-economic Transformation: Limits of Application to post-Soviet Developments

Modernization theory and World System theory are among the most influential theoretical approaches to the problem of socio-economic transformation. Both treat such transformations as movement from a traditional society to an industrial (in the last one hundred and fifty years mostly capitalist) one. A main difference is that Modernization theory offers an optimistic model of transition from a traditional to an industrialized and modern social and economic system. In World System theory, exposure of the less developed countries to the world capitalist system leads to their social and economic stagnation with development of only those sectors of economy which are profitable for the "core" capitalist countries. If Modernization theory projects development of a market economy and democracy in those countries which have embarked upon a path of industrial development, World System theory, by contrast, maintains that underdeveloped peripheral countries are forcibly confined to lower stages of development by the "core" capitalist countries and this entails economic stagnation and dictatorial political regimes. Both World System Theory and the most common interpretation of Modernization Theory stress structural elements, particularly the economic system, as main factors of social transformation.

Theoretically speaking, I am going to test the relevance of these approaches to the recent and current changes in the Soviet-type societies of Eastern Europe and the former USSR. No attempts will be made to undertake a rigorous testing of these theories in their entirety. Rather, I shall look into the validity of their assumptions and corollaries for these particular cases. Although a detailed discussion is yet to be undertaken, at this point I would like to express some reservations about the applicability of these theories to the explanation of both the origins and the outcomes of transformations in the Soviet and post-Soviet societies. Let me tentatively outline some important elements and conditions of the transformation process endemic in these societies which might make it difficult to apply some of the above mentioned theoretical frameworks.

The starting point for recent transformations in the countries of Eastern Europe and the former Soviet Union was not on the level of unindustrialized, traditional societies with relatively simple social structures. All these countries had passed through several stages of industrialization and reached a high degree of differentiation of their social structures with large and complex institutional frameworks. Both Modernization Theory and World System Theory derive their conclusions from the experience of those countries which started as traditional societies and proceeded toward higher levels of social differentiation, economic development, and industrialization. Therefore, they deal with social forces, institutions, and environments quite different from those existing in the countries which are the subject of this research, and it is not implausible to assume that their explanatory and predictive power regarding these countries would be much more limited than on their original grounds.

Of course, former socialist countries of Eastern Europe and the former Soviet Union started their development from traditional to modern industrialized societies in a fashion similar to many other countries. However, under Communist control their development acquired a very specific shape and as such would fit only the most general versions of the theories mentioned above. There were attempts to downplay differences and concentrate instead on similarities of industrial development in socialist and capitalist countries. They were based on a comparison of structural elements and changes in socialist and capitalist countries, such as urbanization, industrialization, growth of large industrial organizations, etc. Convergence Theory, closely related to Modernization Theory, is the most well-known of such attempts. However, in the seventies and especially eighties, when socialist countries missed the next step of industrial development and their technological lag became apparent, Convergence Theory had lost its influence. The attention once again shifted back to specific features of the Soviet-type economic and social systems. This research was mostly carried out by the scholars working within Soviet and East European area studies who did not make extensive use of either of the two main developmental paradigms. Neither Modernization Theory nor World System Theory concentrated on the peculiar structure of property rights in the centrally controlled economy or relations between state and society typical of the late totalitarian and post-totalitarian countries. Since these two aspects of the Soviet-type society were crucial for understanding its difference from capitalist socio-economic system, the two dominant developmental paradigms were seen to be of limited use by students of Soviet-type socio-economic systems.

Both Modernization and World System Theories operate within a context of long-term socio-economic changes.[11] Recent transformations in Eastern Europe and the former Soviet Union seem so rapid and all-embracing that it is not uncommon to refer to them as revolutions. Habermas introduced the term "rectifying revolution" to describe the developments in Eastern Europe (but not in the former Soviet Union). He suggests that these developments present themselves "as a revolution that is to some degree flowing backwards, one that clears the ground in order to catch up with developments previously missed out." (Habermas, 1990, p. 5). As to the nature of this revolution, as well as the developments it is catching up with, Habermas describes them as "a return to old, national symbols" and "the continuation of the political traditions and party organizations of the interwar years" (Ibid.). We will test this approach in later chapters, in discussion of the transformation process in Poland and the Baltics.

World System Theory: Marxism on the World Scale

The Marxist approach can be traced in World System Theory and, to some extent, in Dependency Theory. Both operate within the Marxian frame of reference where concepts of class and exploitation occupy a central place. Both share a historical-materialistic assumption about material factors as the driving force of social change. Interpretations of historical materialism may vary. For example, the leading World System theorist Immanuel Wallerstein rejects the orthodox Marxist vision of socio-economic development as a rigid sequence of stages. However, he does not dispute the materialist conception of history and, not without satisfaction, points out that the majority of World System and Dependency theorists embrace the Marxist tradition (Wallerstein, 1984, p. 122). Wallerstein himself believes that the capitalist market works in accordance with the principles defined by Marx in Volume One of *Capital* (Wallerstein, 1984a, pp. 126-127).[12] World System Theory and Dependency theory take the Marxist assertion about capitalist exploitation being determined by relations and forces of production, and, with some modifications and elaborations, apply it to relations between countries. In this vision, socio-economic transformations are determined by economic factors operating on the international scale. Changes within a country are attributed almost exclusively to the influence of the world capitalist system, internal factors being only reflection of this influence.[13] Tony Smith points out the close affinity between Marxist methodology and that of World System and Dependency theories. "Wallerstein approvingly cites George Lukacs and says that a central tenet of Marxist historiography is that the study of society should "totalize", or begin with an understanding of the whole. Working from this perspective, Wallerstein declares: "The only kind of social system is a world system, which we define quite simply as a unit with a single division of labor and multiple cultural systems." (Smith, 1981, p. 137). One can see that not only economic determinism but also a focus on international level finds a justification in Marxist theory and methodology.

This materialist and determinist approach to social transformation deliberately excludes values and legitimation from considerations or relegates them to a secondary role. This hardly can help in explaining the collapse of the Soviet empire where conflicting national, cultural, and religious values played and continue to play a salient role. I do not intend to reject any of the above approaches at the outset, but it is clear that they require some testing within the context of my research. My intention is, first, to look at whether the emerging legitimation patterns and value orientations fit into the general image of a market economy and democratic society as presented by Modernization theory or into the "core" or "periphery" society as they are described in Dependency theory, and, second, whether an essentially materialist approach possesses sufficient explanatory and predictive power without reference to values and legitimation. Perhaps a more flexible combination of theoretical approaches may be needed to explain phenomena of the post-Communist world.

Modernization Theory Vs. World System Theory: A Comparative Analysis

For many years Modernization Theory served as the most potent explanatory tool in analysis of socio-economic transformation. When this transformation was predominantly seen as proceeding from traditional social systems to modern economies and societies with high degree of differentiation, the theory provided adequate explanations of developmental process both on the theoretical and the empirical level. However, in the mid-sixties it ran into criticism which has continued ever since. Resurgence of crisis tendencies in the post-war developed capitalist societies, attenuation of Western influence in the Third World countries, and, above all, the apparent success of Communist countries in both domestic and international affairs contributed to the emergence of other theories of social transformation. Their approaches were based on theoretical and methodological premises very different from those of Modernization Theory, and they projected a much less optimistic path of socio-economic development.

Modernization Theory was criticized for being what its opponents perceived as an apology for capitalism and Eurocentrism. They pointed out to its failure to recognize imparities in the power distribution among countries as well as its unilinear vision of progress. Consequently, a new theoretical approach was designed to accommodate the socio-political and economic trends of the sixties. World System Theory, the main rival of Modernization

Theory, expanded the Marxist vision of society beyond the borders of one state and into international system. It perceived the world as a hierarchy of the dominated and the dominating, the exploiters and the exploited. Contrary to Modernization Theory, it maintained that the Western path of development associated with democracy and a free market cannot and should not be taken as a guiding example by the less developed countries. According to World System Theory and its more limited version, Dependency Theory, close contacts between developed capitalist and developing countries bred economic stagnation, political corruption and social discontent.[14] These processes result in "anti-systemic movements" whose most visible manifestations are wars of national liberation, often taking on a socialist and Marxist form.

The very existence of the Soviet Union had tremendous symbolic significance for World System Theory. Theoretically, it explicitly based many of its premises on Leninism, the official Soviet ideology.[15] Wallerstein uses not only Lenin's theory of imperialism (which shares major premises with theories of Hobson and, to a lesser extent, Luxembourg), but his theory of the state and class conflict as well. For its empirical evidence World System Theory relied heavily on "anti-systemic" (i.e., anti-Western, anti-capitalist, and often ostensibly pro-Soviet and socialist) movements,[16] many of which would not have succeeded without the direct Soviet help.[17] Even though for Wallerstein the USSR was not anti-systemic enough to be regarded separately from the capitalist-dominated world system, it was nonetheless an important factor in the emergence of genuine anti-systemic movements.[18] Finally, the Soviet Union served as a proof that the free market and democracy do not constitute conditions necessary for a backward "semi-periphery" society to emerge as a military (and, as many liked to believe, economic) superpower capable of being "the counterpoint to American hegemony" (Wallerstein, 1984a, p. 181).

Consequently, the demise of the Soviet Union as well as the Soviet-dominated societies in Eastern Europe and the movement of the Soviet-supported political regimes in the Third World away from their initial goals of socialist development, delivered a major blow to the credibility of crucial postulates of World System Theory.[19] At the same time, the main postulates of Modernization Theory once again seemed to be vindicated in scholarly discourse and practical decision-making.[20] However, Modernization Theory represents a large and complex body of knowledge which lends itself to diverse interpretations. In its application to post-Soviet developments it is sometimes used in a selective and often simplified way and often conflated with the Utilitarian-Positivist approach. This is especially true for empirical studies and recommendations for policy decisions.

Modernization Theory: Interpretations and Applications

Modernization Theory is closely associated with the theoretical works of Talcott Parsons. Some authors, e.g. Mouzelis (1993) and Mueller (1992), credit his theory with an accurate prediction of the collapse of the Soviet socio-economic and political system. The interpretation of Parsons' analysis of Soviet-type societies by these authors is based primarily on the notion of differentiation and adaptive capacity of social system. The argument proceeds from the premise that in order to develop and achieve higher levels of complexity society must increase its capacity to adapt to the changing environment which in turn requires increasing level of differentiation (Mouzelis, 1993, p. 147). Since the Soviet-type society, although with substantially complex and modern industrial system, lacks differentiation of its political system, it has to differentiate the latter in order to proceed towards a full-scale modernity. A higher differentiation of the political system implies the emergence of democratic institutions, diverse spectrum of political parties, and participation of general public in political process. Mouzelis quotes Parsons' prediction that "[communist totalitarian organization] will prove to be unstable and will either make adjustments in the general direction of electoral democracy and a plural party system or "regress" into generally less advanced and politically less effective forms of organization, failing to advance as rapidly or as far as otherwise may be expected." (Parsons, 1964, p. 356, quoted in Mouzelis, 1993, p. 147).

Klaus Mueller interprets one of the main premises of Modernization Theory in the following way: "all societies, falling within the world market's sphere of influence, world political interests or simply Western culture, develop a universal developmental pattern" (Mueller, 1992, p. 111). This pattern includes two major mutually reinforcing components: economic growth (in an essentially market economy) and political democratization.

The above interpretations of Modernization Theory and Parsons' theoretical contribution to its development place them within Utilitarian-Positivist tradition. It presents a model of social change which is purposeful, predictable, and based on rational calculations and comparisons with a superior (in this case Western) socio-economic system. Social change is prompted by the realization that society lacks adaptive capacity (i.e. ability to absorb and process resources from the environment) vis-a-vis other social systems. Society seems to have a choice: either to increase differentiation of its political system thus matching it with already differentiated economy and enter the ranks of more advanced societies, or to retain the existing level of differentiation of the political system and lag behind in its adaptive capacity (in other words, economic efficiency).

Obviously, such a model fails to address several important questions. One of these questions is: who is assessing adaptive capacity and comparing it to that of other societies? In other words: who and on what grounds decides when the time has come for more structurally differentiated social system? The above interpretation of Parsons' theory of differentiation leads us to believe that a rapid increase in the level of structural differentiation as a response to low adaptive capacity is consciously undertaken by a group of reformers who want to increase efficiency of their social system and are well aware of causes and consequences of their actions. This Utilitarian-Positivist reading of Modernization Theory was not uncommon before the collapse of the Soviet Union[21] and became a major methodological foundation for the analysis of post-Soviet developments. However, its shortcomings become apparent if we consider the actual path of the late Soviet and post-Soviet transformation.

If we apply this model to the late Soviet and post-Soviet developments, we can see that it does not explain them satisfactorily. In the model, political democratization should be undertaken to increase economic efficiency. Most post-Soviet societies are by any standard more democratic than the old Communist political system. They possess plural party systems, legislative bodies elected by popular vote, institutionalized public participation in the political process -- none of these phenomena were present under the old regime. However, the first steps toward democratization and mass political participation started before the collapse of the Soviet system. Thus, differentiation of the political system, instead of increasing efficiency of the old regime, seems to have contributed to its eventual breakdown. Many societies emerging after the breakdown have not yet achieved the level of economic efficiency of the old system.

Do the authors discussed above adequately represent the main premises of Modernization Theory or are they just providing one of its interpretations based only on some elements of the theory? In other words, can Modernization Theory be regarded as a part of the Utilitarian-Positivist tradition or there is more to it than simply structural differentiation driven by the efficiency considerations? It is interesting to note that Parsons, whose works are generally seen as the main foundation of Modernization Theory, has been frequently criticized by his opponents for attributing an exaggerated role to value-systems in social continuity and change (e.g. Skocpol, 1979). However, both Mouzelis and Mueller credit him with a correct prediction of the collapse of the Soviet-type societies made from the standpoint of structural differentiation and without explicit reference to the value-system. What is the place of cultural variables in Parsons' vision of social change and how is it incorporated into Modernization Theory? A brief discussion that follows will deal with these questions.

Even a brief look at Parsons' theory of social differentiation casts doubts on the plausibility of its utilitarian interpretation. According to Parsons, all social systems undergo a process of structural differentiation. Some of them differentiate faster than others. Those with lower degree of differentiation can be considered archaic and possess lesser adaptive capacity compared to more differentiated (and therefore more "advanced or "modern") societies. The process of differentiation continues over long periods of time. Even so called "evolutionary breakthroughs" (relatively rapid changes in differentiation patterns that open new possibilities for further advance) take decades and sometimes centuries.[22]

Thus, Parsons' theory of differentiation depicts long-term historical developments rather than actions whose causal effects can be observed in a relatively short time span. Therefore, it cannot be plausibly used for an analysis of reform processes that imply conscious actions (although, as we shall see later, not necessarily with predictable outcomes) and take less than a decade. Parsons' prediction regarding changes in the former Soviet socio-economic system was not and could not be sufficiently specific to explain current transformations in post-Soviet societies. In this prediction Parsons stated that Soviet social system "will prove to be unstable and will either make adjustments in the general direction of electoral democracy and a plural party system or "regress" into generally less advanced and politically less effective forms of organization, failing to advance as rapidly as otherwise may be expected." (Parsons, 1964, p. 356). The statement was intended to indicate that the Soviet system is less advanced, less differentiated than Western capitalist societies and if political differentiation does not occur, its economic efficiency will diminish. Parsons clearly did not attempt to tie this prediction to any particular time frame or to make specific statements as to the shape and pace of the transformation.

Parsons did not perceive structural differentiation as being driven exclusively by structural factors. Alexander writes that in Parsons' model of social change "differentiation is initiated by social strain, which Parsons defines as any force that disrupts the relation between a unit and its environment. Strain can originate from any dimensional source -- from economic, political, integrative, *or cultural* factors." (Alexander, 1983, p. 135, italics added). In *Economy and Society* Parsons and Smelser agree with Durkheim's assertion that economic transformation is not driven by desire for higher efficiency: "Durkheim, in the *Division of Labor* and in *Suicide* held that "happiness" cannot increase cumulatively in the long run, and that the desire for happiness could not be the primary dynamic factor in social change. His statements were couched in the utilitarian terminology of the 1890s. But in our terms he may be interpreted to have stated a denial that a "propensity" to increase the standard of living can serve as the main dynamic force in economic development." (Parsons and Smelser, 1956, pp. 290-291). This statement clearly indicates that Parsons deliberately distanced himself from the Utilitarian-Positivist tradition.

Thus, even a brief examination of Parsons' treatment of structural differentiation suggests that it is implausible to attribute the emergence of Utilitarian-Positivist direction in Modernization Theory to Parsons' influence. It would be equally implausible to place the whole of Modernization Theory within the Utilitarian-Positivist tradition. Such scholars as Robert Bellah, Henry Aujac, David McClelland, and Alex Inkeles share the main premises of Modernization Theory: that societies moving from traditional to modern social systems do exhibit some similar patterns of development. At the same time, they maintain that culture and value-systems play an important role in the developmental process and account for significant variations in speed and patterns of development.

Modernization Theory cannot be plausibly regarded as an epitome of Utilitarian-Positivist tradition of social change. Its theoretical foundations emerged in polemics with neoclassical economics where this tradition finds its most consistent reflection. The way post-Soviet developments are treated by the mainstream Western economics is discussed below.

Post-Soviet Developments and Neoclassical Economics

Not surprisingly, the mainstream economists tend to perceive the collapse of the Soviet system and subsequent developments as economic process *par excellence*. For many years they pointed out the inferior economic performance of the centrally planned economy and its inability to provide sufficient technological innovations (e.g., Kornai, 1990, 1992). The collapse of the Soviet-type economies (STE) validated their (to a large extent abstract theoretical) assertions by making available information on the actual state of affairs in the socialist economies. It should be pointed out that theoretical reasoning about the inefficiency of the STE, although proven correct by the recent developments, should not be taken to correctly predict the systemic collapse of Soviet-type economies and societies. The plausibility of some corollaries derived from the fact of low performance of the STE and its eventual collapse is less obvious. These corollaries include the following: the collapse of the Soviet socio-economic and political system is attributed to the inefficiency of the STE (e.g., Easterly and Fisher, 1994); transition of post-Soviet economies to the essentially market system will occur very rapidly if only guidance and advice are provided by the Western economic experts (Nordhaus, 1991; Sachs and Lipton, 1991).

This approach is employed by the proponents of what David Stark called "capitalism by design" (Stark, 1994, p. 115). Their approach is based on two main assumptions: that the post-Soviet economy, distorted by decades of centralized control, will "naturally" gravitate toward the market; and that the reformist governments in their assistance to the emergence of the market have and will be able to use the perfect knowledge (supplied by the experts) about economic policies and their outcomes.[23]

Despite the lack of positive evidence, the collapse of centrally planned economies and non-democratic societies was perceived by the majority of Western economists as the first step toward replication of Western market and democratic institutions. Post-Soviet socio-economic transformations were repeatedly referred to as transition, implying that both the starting point and the final destination of the process were known in advance (the latter was supposed to be a socio-economic model closely resembling that of developed capitalist countries). Assistance provided by foreign governments and international organizations was designed to direct transitional societies toward this outcome. Blueprints for such assistance included a new Marshall Plan for post-Soviet countries (Sachs, 1990; Welfens, 1992, p. 200) and suggestions about plausibility of importing Western socio-economic institutions into post-Communist societies.

Proponents of the rapid transition by design had a particular view on the distribution of "progressive" and "reactionary" forces in transitional societies. According to this view, Soviet societies were governed by the Communist ruling elites primarily by means of coercion or threat of coercion. Once the oppressive Communist regimes have been replaced by reform-minded democratic governments, the majority of the population would act in favor of a market economy and a democratic polity closely resembling Western socio-economic and political system.

The model of post-Soviet socio-economic transformation created by the proponents of "capitalism by design" manifests a clear affinity with the Utilitarian-Positivist tradition.[24] It is utilitarian because it is based on assumption that people always act rationally in pursuit of their calculable self-interest. It is positivist because it asserts that transition to market economy is predictable, controllable, and can be accomplished by a government whose actions are based on modern economic science. The model itself is simple. Once the reformers gain power, they start the transitional process by rapidly changing the structure of property rights and transferring state-owned assets to private owners. Interestingly, the proponents of market-driven transition attribute an ability to conduct sweeping changes to the same central bureaucracy whose inefficiency in routine management of an old economic system has been clearly demonstrated.

Among the many variants of the existing market economic systems proponents of "capitalism by design" clearly favor the laissez-faire model which implies self-sufficiency of the market with negligible involvement of the state. However, if the target system is the epitome of economic liberalism, transition to it is viewed by its advocates as entailing a series of government actions, consciously undertaken and faultlessly executed. A good illustration of this attitude can be found in the Economic Reform and Integration Project conducted by the International Institute for Applied Systems Analysis. The project dealt with transformation processes in the USSR (the work was completed after the breakdown of the Soviet Union). Its main ideas were published in the book whose title, *What is to be done: Proposals for the Soviet transition to the market*, was indicative of extremely activist stance of the authors. Perhaps it was reflected most clearly in the concluding statements by Kimio Uno: "it is useful to summarize the primary thesis of this book. This is a manifesto for economic reform, although it is stated in the sober prose of economics. The sober, straightforward prose does not lessen the urgency of the manifesto's message. In 1902, Lenin borrowed the title *What Is To Be Done?* from the nineteenth-century novel by Chernyshevskii, and we have elected to borrow it from him. In his book, Lenin emphasized the importance of a vanguard party -- his soon to be formed Bolshevik party -- in leading the masses to revolution. In some sense, Lenin's *What Is To Be Done?* provided much of the organizational framework for the events that followed. We claim no similar historical import for the chapters of this small volume. Yet it is true that, without some logical and consistent program, the Soviet transition to the market is impossible. And for that *we can see no alternative to some form of the proposals put forward here.*" (Uno, 1991, pp. 177-178, italics added).[25]

The proposals put forward in the book, as those introduced by many other scholars, revolved around three main directions of reform: stabilization, liberalization, and privatization. The authors insisted that "the only effective approach is to have a *complete and simultaneous systemic change* to the market" (Nordhaus, 1991, p. 93, italics in the original) without even discussing the government's ability or willingness to implement such a change. Advocates of such a state-introduced capitalism may argue about details of transition (such as sequencing of principal steps of reforms, mechanisms of privatization, monetary policies, etc.), but they share the same pragmatic position: transition leads to the market, and they know how the market works. Therefore, theoretical questions are considered to have already been solved and the emphasis is on practical reforms. Jeffrey Sachs describes his career as an economic adviser to post-Soviet governments as "life in the economic emergency room", where specific issues of reforms should be swiftly and forcefully attended to (Sachs, 1994). The metaphor of the emergency room evokes the image of a totally passive patient (the economy) completely dependent upon the doctor (the economic expert). Another, even more famous, metaphor, that of "shock therapy", has similar meaning.[26]

Views of the radical economists on economic transformation can be concisely expressed with the help of mathematical formulae widely used in econometrics. Hans-Juergen Wagener proposes the following model of economic transition:

$$Y = f(E,S,P) \tag{1}$$
$$S = (R,O) \tag{2}$$

Y denotes a vector consisting of variables used to measure economic performance. It depends upon environment E, economic system S, and strategies P. The economic system includes two basic elements: traditional and customary regularities of behavior R and institutionalized economic order O. If we are able to specify the impact of the order on performance:

$$f = \frac{\partial Y}{\partial O} \tag{3}$$

then it is possible to establish preference of one order over the other. For example, if Om denotes the market order and Oa administrative order and

$$fO_m = \frac{\partial Y}{\partial O_m} > fO_a = \frac{\partial Y}{\partial O_a} \tag{4}$$

then it is rational to abandon Oa and adopt Om (Wagener, 1993, p. 4).

Wagener starts his discussion of institutional transformation with this model and clearly states that other elements (E, R, and P) of the model are held constant. He does not imply that the model adequately reflects the post-Soviet economic transformations. However, this model, precisely in its simplified form seems to dominate the treatment of post-Soviet transformations by the neoclassical economists. Superior economic performance of the market system can be supported by empirical evidence. However, we can only assume that the actor (in this case, the government) can determine what impact a particular economic order has on the performance of the economy. We also should assume that variables comprising vector Y are the same for the market and administrative system, in other words, that these systems have compatible sets of preferences. If they do not, then the target performance will not be associated with the market economic model; instead, the reformers will try to attain their set of preferences by means of some other order which might be impossible to specify. Another assumption is that the target order and corresponding performance can be reached in one step and that the time of transition is negligible. If the above assumptions are true, then notation **(4)** correctly reflects the transitional process. In the discussion that follows in this and the later chapters we are going to analyze the validity of these assumptions.

Measuring Variations of Market Transition

The development of market structures after the collapse of the Soviet-Type Economy (STE) differs in pace and shape from one country to another. In discussing the above paradigms I will test their explanatory power with regard to cross-national variations of post-Communist market development. Those theories that explain the variations can be used for creating hypotheses and further analysis.

From both a practical and a theoretical standpoint, the explanation of these differences is quite important. They indicate variations in the balance of pro- and anti-reform forces, combination of the previously existing conditions that may impede or facilitate transition. Above all, they illustrate successes and failures of particular reform policies in particular countries. Theoretically, the importance of variations in the speed and shape of transitions is even more pronounced since it presents an opportunity for testing various theoretical approaches. If a particular theory is able to explain these variations, then its premises could be considered valid. On the other hand, a theory which attempts to explain a particular development but fails to account for cross-national variations does not possess sufficient explanatory power. Before the comparison, however, we should clarify some methodological questions related to measurement of socio-economic changes.

Due to imperfect information, exact measurement of a market progress is impossible and any comparison necessarily will be crude.[27] However, apart from these difficulties there exist more profound methodological and conceptual problems. Should we regard the recent changes in the economies of the post-Communist states as movements toward a market, or as departures from a highly centralized economy that may or may not be directed toward a modern capitalist market? If we accept the latter view, then we need to measure a movement *away* from the centralized economy. The measurement in the latter case is relatively simple. All we have to know is to what degree the previous system of centralized planning and control over individual enterprises has been dismantled. The relinquishing of centralized control does eliminate the previous economic system but does not tell us what kind of system is emerging in its place. To measure the progress *toward* the market, we have to present a model, however abstract, of the market economic system.

It is surprising that the discipline of economics, although tacitly assuming the existence of markets (or, rather, a particular sort of market), does not have a substantially detailed discussion of these institutions. This peculiarity has been pointed out by Richard Swedberg (1994, p. 257) and earlier   by Douglass North (1977, p. 710). As these authors note, neo-classical economic thought does contain descriptions of the market as a price-regulating mechanism but stops short of discussing its substantive features as a social institution. In order to facilitate research on the market as a system of relations (rather than simply an instrument for the most efficient price setting),[28] Ronald Coase proposes to define the market as a "social institution that facilitates exchange" (1988, p. 8). Emphasis on exchange and allocation of scarce resources through competitive price-setting is central for the concept of the market in neo-classical economics. Though the concept is adequate for purely economic research, it leaves unanswered questions about some substantively important features of markets as well as about non-economic conditions necessary for them to function. These characteristics and conditions are especially interesting for the students of the economies in transition from a predominantly non-market to a predominantly market system.

Adopting a synthetic concept of the market as a system of competitive exchange, Swedberg proposes an ideal type of the modern capitalist market which includes the following main elements: free competition (national and international), competition in the market as well as competition in production, competitive behavior deeply rooted in society, rational mechanisms to facilitate the exchange (low search costs); bargaining only at the margin; full machinery of the modern state to back up the exchange (low enforcement costs) (1994, p. 273).

This ideal type is compatible with market concepts in neoclassical economics but also delineates key social conditions necessary for the emergence and functioning of a modern capitalist market. I would like to stress that economic competition as a means of seeking economic gains is of course the most important element of modern markets, whereas the use of non-economic means to achieve economic gains leads to monopolistic and inefficient markets and is indicative of the lack of ability (or willingness) of the state to create a market environment.

Following the ideal type proposed by Swedberg, we can introduce several key variables reflecting progress toward a modern market economy. First is the number of bankruptcies. Provided that real economic competition exists, low economic efficiency is likely to have very tangible consequences for the enterprises: they either reorganize and increase efficiency or disappear through the institutionalized mechanism of bankruptcy. Transitional economies inherited many enterprises that are inefficient and unlikely to withstand a real competition. Therefore, the number of bankruptcies would indicate the extent to which economic competition actually has become a part of economic environment.

A second related indicator is the absence of entry barriers to the economy for newcomers, both domestic and foreign. Thus, the number of newly emerging private firms (including small privatization discussed below) along with indicators showing the attractiveness of the economy to foreign investors (as well as the actual volume of direct foreign investments) should be important measures of market progress. Obviously, the existence of high entry barriers serve mostly political purposes, such as the protection of industries with politically strong constituencies (regardless of their efficiency) and does not facilitate economic competition.

What indicators can be used to measure the state's facilitation of exchange process? Of course, facilitation of exchange by lowering enforcement costs may be reflected in the recorded rates of organized criminal activity linked to various types of extortion by requiring "protection" payments from the entrepreneurs. The higher the extortion rates, the less successful the state is in reducing enforcement costs. These data, however, are not easily available and often unreliable. Besides, they reflect only a fraction of total enforcement costs and do not reflect search costs at all. The existing structure of government agencies charged with the task of facilitating exchange through lowering search and enforcement costs for individual actors, as well as the legal framework constructed for these purposes, indicate only the potential ability of the state to facilitate exchange and not the actual state of affairs. The direct analysis of institutions for facilitation of market exchange is hampered by the lack of information and by the general ambiguity of the transition period when many institutions do not yet function properly, not because of a lack of willingness, but because of insufficient experience.

There is one element of a market economy which provides a very good indicator of how far the state actually reduces transaction costs for individual actors (without necessarily taking part of the costs upon itself). This is the changing amount of money in circulation and, subsequently, the rate of inflation. If the latter is high, the predictability of outcomes of economic transactions decreases, which significantly raises transaction costs. High inflation discourages investments which in the long run are essential for a successful transition and recovery. In the shorter run, it makes for a lack of confidence in money as a medium of exchange and forces economic actors to resort more to barter with increasing search and enforcement costs. Hyperinflation breeds growing inflationary expectations which acquire a life of their own and can become a major source of economic as well as social and political instability. A hyperinflationary economy moves away from the ideal type of the modern market and toward an economic system where economic competition is replaced by political bargaining of organized interest groups, which makes transaction costs inordinately high for each individual actor thus diverting resources from productive use. All this may sound commonplace for anyone familiar with the basic principles of economics, but policies of many post-Soviet governments indicate that they have not yet learned to appreciate the dangers of inflation.

The lower the inflation rate in a transitional economy, the closer the state is to its role in the ideal-typical model. Successful anti-inflationary measures also indicate the existence of broad social and political conditions for the transition to a market economy. A tight monetary policy means that the main beneficiaries of the Communist direct subsidies and post-Communist inflationary distributions are at a disadvantage. The main groups that have benefitted from inflation in the past are industrial workers and managers of large state-owned and subsidized enterprises who always took their job and income security for granted. They are likely to be well organized and capable of concerted and sustained anti-government action. The fact that under these conditions they do not use their strength to change the government policy of market transition indicates that the state enjoys substantial legitimacy for its economic policy, even when it goes against the immediate interests of powerful interest groups.[29]

The above indicators point to structural conditions for the emergence and development of a modern capitalist market economy. However, in our analysis we are concerned with a very early stage of market transitions in different countries. Given the short time elapsed since the collapse of the Soviet-type economies, it is too early to tell toward what kind of market these economies are moving. At this point, it is much more important to know the speed of their movement away from the centrally planned economic system. For this purpose an aggregate indicator is needed.

There are three indicators currently used for measurement of the market transformation in the former centrally planned economies. One is the number of privately-owned enterprises (or the increase in this number) in a particular economy. Another is a synthetic indicator constructed on the basis of several other indicators[30] and presented as a numerical score on a scale from one to ten (or five). The higher the score, the more successful is market transition. The third indicator is a share of GDP produced by privately-owned enterprises.

The main advantage of the first indicator is that it shows an actual number of primary economic units that are not subject to central control and operate as independent actors within a market system. This information is important. However, since many of the newly emerging enterprises are small, and -- being new and small -- unstable, many of them disappear shortly after they have emerged. The indicator does not distinguish between viable enterprises that have existed for some time and those just registered and with uncertain future. What's more, since these enterprises vary in size, their number does not indicate their importance for the overall performance of the economy.

Different types of scores are used mostly by international organizations, such as the World Bank or IMF. The synthetic nature of these indicators allows them to include not only quantitative but also qualitative information. The main disadvantage is that there is no universally accepted procedure of calculating these scores. Every agency includes different information in them and gives different weights to different constituent parts of the score. The reasons for these differences are unclear, and indicators of this type produced by different agencies are incompatible and there is no obvious reason to prefer one of them over others. Therefore, this type of indicators does not allow a comparison of estimates made by different agencies to be clear and consistent.

The share of GDP produced by the private sector is one indicator that gives a clear, albeit simplified, picture of market transformation. Although it provides only a crude measurement and tells nothing about the ways and conditions which may account for a particular outcome, it is sufficient for preliminary ranking of countries in terms of their progress in dismantling of the old economic system. It indicates the strength of the private sector economy vis-a-vis the part of economic system remaining under the state control.

In the discussion that follows we will use the share of GDP produced by the private sector as the main criterion of market transformations in cross-national comparisons. According to the European Bank for Reconstruction and Development, in 1994 55 percent of Poland's GDP was produced in the private sector; the figure was the same for Latvia and Estonia, and slightly lower for Lithuania (50 percent). At the same time, in Belarus only 15 percent of GDP was produced in the private sector.[31] These figures can be taken as an indication of successful market transition in Poland and the three Baltic states and lack of such a transition in Belarus. How would theories described earlier in this chapter account for these differences?

Theories of Socio-Economic Transformation: Models and Hypotheses

World System Theory

The dependent variable in our discussion is the speed of market transition. In the context of World System Theory this transition is expressed in terms of capitalist development, more precisely, a movement away from an essentially non-capitalist economy which is relatively isolated from the world capitalist system toward inclusion into this system.

Consequently, in the frame of reference of World System theory the main independent variable would be the influence of the world capitalist system. In what forms does world capitalism exercise its influence over the peripheral and semi-peripheral countries? In other words, how can we make the variable operational? Apparently, there are two main ways for the core capitalist countries to influence less advanced economies and keep them within their sphere of influence: foreign trade and foreign investments (both direct and as in the form of loans).

World System Theory presents the following model of capitalist development of the newly independent states. "The states and the nations are both creations resulting from the ongoing process of the world economy. They are not only created institutions; they are institutions that are being constantly re-created. The states are defined by and constrained by their necessary relationship to a state-structure. The problem for the accumulators of capital is that they need to utilize state-structures as a crucial intervening mechanism in the construction and constant reconstruction of the world market. In order, however, to do that, they have to foster nationalism as the social glue of these structures." (Wallerstein 1984a, p. 134). In this quotation Wallerstein does acknowledge a role of nationalism in socio-economic transformations.

However, nationalism in his interpretation is not a relatively independent indigenous phenomenon. Instead, nationalism is encouraged and advanced by the dominant forces in the world economy ("accumulators of capital") in order to gain access to local markets. Indeed, nations themselves are seen as creations of the world economy, a mere by-product of capitalist economic expansion. The statement is logically consistent with the main postulates of World System Theory that in the orthodox Marxist fashion affirms the primacy of economy over society and regards local processes as derivations of the general and universal trends in the capitalist world economy.

The above model leads to the following hypothesis about the cross-national differences in market transition: countries with higher levels of foreign trade and foreign investments prior to the collapse of the Soviet system will move toward the Western community of nations and the capitalist market economy faster than those countries with smaller amounts of foreign trade and foreign investments. How does this hypothesis apply to the five countries in our study?

If we confine our comparison to Poland and Belarus, then it might seem that the hypothesis is correct. Indeed, Poland in the seventies and eighties attracted substantial foreign loans from private and international financial institutions. These funds were used to import capital equipment and consumer goods. The former was primarily intended for the development of export-oriented industries. Nothing on a comparable scale occurred in Belarus. So far, the hypothesis holds. However, it does not seem as plausible if we add that nothing on a comparable scale occurred in Latvia, Lithuania, and Estonia. In fact, their foreign trade was indistinguishable from that of Belarus (since all four countries were Soviet republics and as such were subject to the centrally designed and conducted foreign trade policy). However, all three Baltic states are at least as successful as Poland in dismantling the old economic system (actually, Estonia has been even more successful).

There is yet another part of the transition process where World System Theory does not adequately represent reality. According to this theory, the active role in expanding the capitalist world system belongs to the core capitalist countries. Therefore, if some countries are incorporated into the capitalist system earlier than others, one of the primary reasons would be that the former are more attractive to the core countries ("accumulators of capital") than the latter. In our case, prior to the collapse of the Soviet Union the three Baltic republics would be more attractive to world capitalism than Belarus. World System Theory maintains that the core countries seek to include other countries into the capitalist system because of potential for exploitation of their natural resources and cheap labor force. Once again, this explanation does not hold for Belarus and the Baltic states. All four countries share the same scarcity of natural resources and roughly the same cost and composition of labor force. Thus, none of them is more attractive than the others from the standpoint of World System Theory.

Even the above brief discussion indicates that World System Theory does not adequately explain the differences in post-Soviet economic transformation. Therefore, the hypothesis based on the premises of this theory should be rejected.

Ad Hoc Pragmatic Approach

The dependent variable in this framework is market development. The market is seen as a replica of Western capitalist markets which in turn are seen as networks of free exchange of resources unfettered by outside interference.

The independent variable is democratization and increased political participation. It is seen as a means to abolish the Communist oppression and allow the reformist government to come to power. The assumption is that people in Communist societies always were in favor of the market economy and, once they were given a chance, will vote for those politicians who promise to conduct market reforms.

The above view stressed universality of the market transition. It was not concerned with the in-depth explanation of the differences between the speed and shape of these transformations among different countries. Characteristically, those authors who attempted such explanations were quite critical about the approach to market transition as imitation of the existing capitalist institutions (e.g. Stark, 1994).

Since there is not a single post-Communist country where market transition has gone fully according to the prescribed models, proponents of "capitalism by design" had to come up with some explanation. Marie Lavigne provides the following summary of such explanations: "generally, the final aim being a "fully-fledged" market, whatever goes wrong during the process is attributed: (i) to the legacies of the past; (ii) to a wrong evaluation of the reality due to imperfect statistics; (iii) to technical errors in policies; and ultimately (iv) to the inadequate assistance of the West" (Lavigne, 1995, p. 249). Interestingly, each of these explanations undermines the validity of a particular assumption used to build the model of transition. Explanation (iv) contradicts the assumption of the self-sustaining market development. Explanations (ii) and (iii) contradict assumptions of perfect knowledge possessed by the experts and the reformist governments. Since explanation (i) questions the crucial assumption about the willingness of the reformist government to conduct market reforms, it deserves further elaboration.

When the radical economists analyze failures of reform processes the main culprit is considered to be the resistance of the old Communist bureaucracy. Consequently, the cross-national differences in speed of socio-economic transformations are explained in the same way: those countries lagging behind in implementation of reforms have more entrenched and powerful groups of Communist apparatchiks than those that are more success-ful in market transition.

The above hypothesis may be correct. Indeed, the old system of centralized control over the economy proved to be more difficult to dismantle than was originally expected. However, this explanation does not answer why in some countries it proved to be more difficult than in others. Democratic procedures had been introduced in all five countries of our sample shortly after the collapse of Soviet Communism, but in Poland and the Baltic states they brought reformist governments to power, whereas in Belarus the outcome has been quite different. The described approach does not even attempt to explain this difference.

Proponents of "capitalism by design" correctly identified the state apparatus as the main collective actor at the initial stage of market reforms. They were also correct in pointing out the balance between the old and new members of this apparatus as a source of cross-national differences (and imperfections common to all countries) in the speed of transition process. However, the post-factum explanations contradict their initial assumption of the predictability of market transition.

Thus, the hypothesis based on the ad hoc practical approach has serious logical inconsistencies and does not provide a satisfactory explanation of cross-national differences in market transition.

An Alternative Approach: Differences in Cultural and Value-systems May Account for Cross-national Variations of Market Development

The approaches described above concentrate on the structural explanations of socio-economic changes. Each of them does possess sufficient explanatory power in cases of some societies undergoing some type of transformation under some conditions. However, in our case these approaches fail to adequately explain cross-national differences in the speed of market transfor-mation. This may serve as an indication of the unique nature of post-Soviet developments as well as suggest a need for a broader and more flexible combination of theoretical premises.

All the above approaches seek to explain socio-economic transformations by changing distribution of power among the social groups with different material interests. Therefore, one reason for their inadequacy in our case may be the fact that structural conditions that influence distribution of power in all five countries prior to the collapse of the Soviet-type system were quite similar. In the case where key input variables in a model of socio-economic development are similar one cannot expect the model to account for variations of outcomes within the sample.

Neither the Marxist nor the Utilitarian-Positivist frame of reference, with their premises based on materialism, determinism, and predictability, seem to provide adequate theoretical foundations for the explanation of cross-national differences in post-Soviet socio-economic transformations. An alternative approach may lie within the context of the Weberian paradigm of social change. Its broad treatment of the concept of rationality, attention to cultural traits unique to a particular country, as well as the idea that a change of economic order may be an unintended consequence of changes in a social subsystem seemingly unrelated to the economy -- all this provides a frame of reference which helps to introduce a variety of socio-economic phenomena into the analysis. This makes for a more inclusive, and hence a more realistic model of market transformation. Habermas' notion of "catch-up moderniza-tion" falls into this context.

If the structural conditions do not show significant differences, then we should examine other subsystems of societies in our study. Those exhibiting visible differences may be a key to the explanation of cross-national variations of socio-economic changes. Even a brief comparison of the five countries in the sample yields one peculiar phenomenon: if the Baltic states and Poland exhibit a vibrant nationalism (not only as a cultural trait but also as a means to justify policy decisions), Belarus seems to have missed the Springtime of Nations in Eastern Europe. Its reluctant acceptance of independence in 1991 was due to the dissolution of the USSR rather than any conscious attempt to assert its national sovereignty.

Prior to the final collapse of Soviet domination in Poland the country had a well developed civil society which included a multitude of voluntary organizations which varied in size, agenda, and relationship to the Communist state. Two of these organizations, often considered instrumental in the fall of Communism in Poland, were the Solidarity and the Roman Catholic Church. The former had been a center for open and active opposition to the regime for ten years. The latter provided spiritual guidance in tacit opposition to the regime in the post-war years as it did for more than a century of Russian domination before Poland became independent in 1918. The Roman Catholic

Church in Poland became a national, as well as religious, institution and an active participant in political processes.

In Lithuania, the Roman Catholic Church was one of the forces supporting the organized opposition to the Soviet regime. However, the main role in this opposition belonged to organizations with an explicitly nationalist agenda. They started to emerge immediately after the Soviet political system began to lose its oppressive nature in the late eighties. Not only in Lithuania but also in Latvia and Estonia the last years of the Soviet Union were marked by the emergence of mass movements and voluntary organizations whose goals had manifest nationalist overtones.

Started as organizations of intellectuals with an almost exclusively cultural agenda, they rapidly gained strength, attracted followers from all social strata, and included political and economic chapters into their programs. Nationalist opposition in Belarus had been developing along a similar path. However, value-orientations of the general public were quite different.

Among the dozen or so nations which had moved from the strict Communist domination Belarus has been conspicuous by the absence of a widespread nationalist sentiment. Before the collapse of the USSR, Belarus had the political, economic, and social structures typical of a constituent Soviet republic. The most salient feature of its cultural landscape was the successful suppression of the indigenous Byelorussian culture and national identity as a result of a prolonged Russification campaign. Although all religious activities were discouraged, the Russian Orthodox Church was treated much more leniently than the Roman Catholic Church which used to be well established in Belarus before the revolution and, in Western Belarus, before the Soviet intervention in 1939. No one even dreamed of the revival of the Uniate Church which, before its abolition in 1839, was essentially the Byelorussian national institution. A value system devoid of the national and religious components was quite suitable for the ruling elite which did not have to reconcile diverse values with the dominant Communist ideology. However, the legitimation vacuum proved to be a major problem when in 1991 Belarus reluctantly accepted independence which resulted not from conscious attempts to gain it but from the dissolution of the Soviet empire initiated by Russia.

The value system in Belarus may be seen as being centered around two sets of conflicting and competing value-orientations. One value dichotomy is between Communist ideology and central planning and pragmatism and market economy. Another is that between Russian imperialism and national independence. It should be noted that Russian imperialism is promoted not only by the ethnic Russians and organizations with an explicitly Russian imperialist agenda (such as the Slavic Assembly or Officer's Union) but also by many officials in the central as well as local government regardless of their ethnic affiliation. These value-orientations are only loosely interrelated. Nationalism is usually coupled with a very cautious and qualified acceptance of market ideology, whereas peripheral imperialism is combined with advocacy of continuing central economic control.

In the Baltics, the new elites had been brought to power by rise of national consciousness and desire for independence. In Poland, anti-Communism coupled with hostility toward Russian imperialism played a similar role in the circulation of elites. In a sharp contrast both with Poland and the Baltics, Belarus did not experience an advent of nationalist, anti-Russian and anti-Communist elites. We can make a plausible assumption that this difference somehow contributes to variations in market progress among the countries in our sample.

Before we test the validity of this assumption, one more question should be answered. The proponents of "capitalism by design" imply that there are two necessary conditions for a successful market transition. First, the rulers should be committed to the free market economy. Second, the experts should have adequate knowledge of capitalist markets. What if the variations in market transition in our sample are caused by differences in cognitive models of the experts? I will attempt to answer this question in Chapter Two.

Notes

1   These approaches, often serving as a foundation for decision-making relating to economic policies of transition, do not emerge in a theoretical vacuum. Rather, they are based on interpretations and modifications of particular theories.

2   A detailed discussion on interpretations of Marxist historical materialism and retention of core elements despite diversity of interpretations can be found, for example, in *Main Currents of Sociological Thought* by Raymond Aron (1965, vol.1, pp. 189-191)

3   For detailed argument see: Bottomore 1991 and 1993; G. Konrad and I. Szelenyi 1979.

4   They are presented by Bottomore (1993, p. 30) as monolithic groups.

5   Thomas Rigby present the most definite position on the issue of class approach to the Soviet society: "If we understand "class" in narrowly Marxist terms as determined by "relations of production" seen as property relations, "class" would seem to have limited analytical value for a society in which private ownership of the means of production been marginalized. Power, status, and access to goods and services rests on resources other than property resources" (Rigby, T.H. 1990, p. 7).

6   More detailed discussion of Comte's and Spencer's theories is provided by Turner and Beeghley (1982).

7   The main thrust of the "new institutional economics" is to deflect the analysis of institutions from sociological, historical, and legal argumentation and show instead that they arise as the efficient solution to economic problems. This mission and the pervasive functionalism it implies discourage the detailed analysis of social structure that I argue is

the key to understanding how existing institutions arrived at their state" (Granovetter, 1991, p. 505).

8   Parsons considered the Utilitarian and Positivist paradigms to be closely interrelated. According to Parsons, "positivism provides crucial ammunition for an instrumentalist approach to action. The utilitarians, he argues, were not only rationalists but positivists as well" (Alexander, 1983, p. 16).

9   "The conceptual scheme of the classical economics was enabled to flourish as a serious scientific theory precisely because it was applied to a society *in which the basic problem of order was assumed to be solved.* Economic relations as conceived by the classical economics can take place on a significant scale only within a framework of order by virtue of which force and fraud are at least held within bounds and where the rights of others are respected to a degree" (Parsons, 1937 [1968], p. 101, italics added).

10   "Our central proposition is that quantitative changes of a sufficient order of magnitude involve changes of *organization* in the system in question. Furthermore, a change of organization, unless it is confined to the level of segmentation, is a modification of the *structure of the system.* If, therefore, the economy is treated as a social system in the full sense, then the focus of the problem of structural change accompanying and resulting from quantitative growth lies in the system of institutions. But in the general theory of social systems the structure of the system of economic or any other institutions cannot be primarily a function of economic factors, though it is in part determined by them. The problem of structural change in the economy and every other sub-system of the society must, therefore, be treated as a sociological problem. Positive theoretical analysis in this area cannot be confined to economic theory, but must involve the specific interdependence of economic and sociological theory" (Parsons and Smelser, 1956, pp. 246-247; italics in original).

11   I do not intend to say that these theories are concerned exclusively with the long-term processes. They do approach changes occurring in a relatively short time span. However, both Modernization and World System Theory tend to concentrate on long-term evolutionary developments, whereas the rapid socio-economic transformations are of secondary importance in this context.

12   Although Wallerstein concentrates on the study of markets, he does not deviate from Marx's economic theory because he agrees that relations of material production (specifically, the capitalist method of the extraction of surplus value) determine the forms of distribution and exchange (Wallerstein, 1984, p. 15).

13   "If the world system is the focus of analysis, and in particular we are talking of the capitalist world economy, then divergent historical patterns are precisely to be expected. They are not an anomaly but the essence of the system. If the world economy is the basic economic entity comprising a single division of labor, then it is natural that different areas perform different economic tasks. Since, however, political boundaries (states) are smaller than the economic whole, they will each reflect different groupings of economic tasks and strengths in the world market" (Wallerstein, 1984, p. 128).

14   "Underdevelopment was and still is generated by the very same historical process which also generated economic development: the development of capitalism itself." (Frank, 1972, p. 9, quoted in Smith, 1984, p. 136). Arno Tausch is among the scholars who recently pointed out that the World System theory, by placing the blame for economic underdevelopment on world capitalist system shows its close affinity with Marxism (Tausch, 1993, p. 12).

15   It seems that treating Lenin's theories seriously is a must for every World System theorist. For example, Daniel Chirot, then one of proponents of the World System Theory, gives

a sympathetic account of Lenin's theory of imperialism and uses its premises throughout his book *Social Change in the Twentieth Century* (1977, pp. 49-52). Terence Hopkins, another important World System theorist, discusses at length Lenin's theory and methodology as a foundation of the World System analysis (Hopkins, 1982, pp. 149-152).

16   Rhetoric of World System theorists sometimes seems to fit for a *Pravda* editorial. Wallerstein wrote: "The struggle [against capitalism] takes place on all fronts -- political, economic, and cultural -- and in all arenas of the world, in the core states, in the periphery (largely in the Third World), and in the semi-periphery (many but not all of which states have collective ownership of basic property and are hence called "socialist" states" (Wallerstein, 1984, p. 131).

17   Chirot admits that "Soviet aid has been a key ingredient of several successful revolutions" (Op. cit., p. 228).

18   The following statement sums up Wallerstein's view on the position of the USSR vis-a-vis the world system. "The Soviet regime was the product of the Bolshevik Revolution of 1917, a major expression of a steadily expanding network or family of world anti-systemic movements. Although the USSR was not as strong, either economically or militarily, as anyone pretended, it was just strong enough to create world-systemic space for various anti-hegemonic and anti-systemic forces" (Wallerstein, 1984a, p. 135).

19   "The collapse of the Soviet block has meant the disappearance of perhaps the only articulated alternative to the capitalist model. Is it too much to say that we have reached the point where there is no viable concept of development left, except perhaps for the surviving capitalist one which has encountered both practical differences and ideological disaffection in the last third of the century?" (Smelser, 1994, p. 235).

20   A view of the recent post-Soviet developments as a proof of validity of Modernization Theory is expressed e. g. by Mouzelis (1993) and Mueller (1992), although with some reservations by the latter.

21   Rueschemeyer points out a contradiction between utilitarian components of Moderniza-tion Theory and its early Parsonian foundation: "Such a reading underlies in fact much of the recent "modernization theory" -- an ironic turn of intellectual events considering that this theory had its roots in a conception of sociology as the corrective countertradition to individualist utilitarian social theory" (Rueschemeyer, 1986, p. 8).

22   Parsons identifies the following key evolutionary breakthroughs: the emergence of social stratification, cultural differentiation, money and markets, bureaucracy, democratic association. It is clear that each of these phenomena took a considerable time to emerge, develop, and become a fully institutionalized part of social system.

23   There is an important distinction between perfect knowledge and perfect information. Modern economics admits that information available to economic actors is seldom perfect. However, there is a vast economic analytical apparatus designed specifically to cope with problems of uncertainty and imperfect information. On the other hand, actors' knowledge about fundamental principles of economic processes is assumed to be perfect. For example, if information about the money supply in post-Soviet economies is imperfect, analysts must have means to offset these imperfections and produce a figure quite close to reality. However, they do not question the desire of the government to conduct anti-inflationary policy and its understanding of its likely outcomes.

24   It is interesting to note that they seem to have a certain affinity with the Marxist tradition as well. They tend to perceive post-Soviet societies as consisting of two conflicting groups ("reformers" and "reactionaries"), a view closely resembling Marxist class approach (this feature has been noted by Wagener, 1992, p. 15). They insist on revolutionary, that is

sweeping, all-embracing and rapid, changes of the institutional tructure and the structure of property rights. They maintain that socialism has been undermined by its own inefficiency, echoing the Marxist view on the capitalist economy undermined by its own contradictions. However, just as Marx and the Marxists could not say at what precise point these contradictions would lead to capitalism's collapse, proponents of "capitalism by design" cannot say at what particular point of its continuous decline did the inefficiency of socialist economy reach its critically untenable level.

25 This far-fetched analogy seems even more ironic if we consider that the outcome of the Bolshevik revolution deviated significantly from Lenin's original intentions.

26 Jeffrey Sachs, Anders Aslund and other neoclassical economic advisors were correct in identifying causes of inefficiencies of Soviet-type economies. They correctly anticipated that economically efficient reform policies will meet political opposition. The unforeseen outcomes of their policy recommendations stem mostly from the fact that they were the first among Western scholars to address the problem of post-Communist systemic transformation as a practical issue.

27 The following problems are among those precluding exact measurement of market transitions in post-Soviet economies.

(1) The main data sources are official statistics which in many cases are unreliable. They do not adequately reflect the performance of the private sector and tend to inflate the performance of the state-controlled sector. In the latter, goods and services still are indirectly subsidized and centrally distributed, thus making indicators incompatible with those for the private sector.

(2) Different sources provide different information about the same process at the same time.

(3) Sometimes even one source contains mutually contradictory data.

28 According to North, a market is not necessarily the most efficient economic arrangement and contains both efficient and inefficient institutions (North, 1990, p. 69).

29 Of course, this might indicate the strength of the state vis-a-vis its potential opponents. However, in the case of Eastern Europe and the former Soviet Union states were left with much less capacity than their Communist predecessors and cannot rely on an oppressive apparatus to support their economic policies.

30 Such indicators may include the share of GNP produced by private firms, their share of labor force, share of privately owned industrial assets, number of private firms and its yearly increase, etc.

31 *Report on Economic Transition in Eastern Europe and the Former Soviet Union in 1994.* European bank for Reconstruction and Development, London, 1994.

2 Economic Models and Market Images in Scholarly and Political Discourse Prior to the Collapse of the Soviet System

In formulating and executing new economic policies two groups play crucial roles: the decision-makers (political masters in Weber's words) and the experts. The former are of special importance due to their position of power and the latter due to the specialized knowledge and skills they possess. In a post facto study of a social transformation that includes circulation of elites the roles of aspiring rulers and their advisers are equally important.[1] Carsten Hermann-Pillath (1993, p. 113) in his study of socio-economic transition draws attention to values and cognitive models prevailing among the dominant elites as important determinants of the transformation process. In his interpretation, cognitive models include economic theories and social philosophies, as well as value-systems and expectations which actors use to assess costs and benefits of prospective policies. In the course of socio-economic transformation these models exhibit a tendency to incremental change. I would suggest that these cognitive models include administrative experience as yet another element and are structured by patterns of interaction between the rulers and the experts. Drastic changes in these patterns, e.g. in case of circulation of elites, may lead to rapid changes in cognitive models.

A simplified model of interaction between the decision-makers and the experts usually can be presented as a straightforward two-step process. At the first step a policy outline is conveyed by "political masters" to the experts so that they could make a detailed proposal for actual policy. At the second step the experts convey the draft of the policy to the decision-makers who assess its compatibility with the original outline. If political masters are satisfied, the draft becomes a foundation for an actual policy decision, to be implemented by a bureaucratic system. If they are not satisfied, they send the draft back to the experts who make adjustments and repeat step two once again. This type of interaction is typical for routine activities of executive authorities, or reforms that are not intended to change the fundamental systemic characteristics. In this case, cognitive models of both rulers and experts are likely to undergo a gradual, incremental change. As Rueschemeyer and Skocpol (1996, p. 298) pointed out, the knowledge-bearing institutions are not only "influenced by economic, social, and state arrangements; they become reciprocally influential." Over time, this influence shapes what Rueschemeyer and Skocpol call "background assumptions" of policy-makers.[2] In fact, they maintain that social science (and, consequently, bearers of social knowledge) has greater effect on these assumptions than on specific policy decisions (Ibid., p. 308).

Of course, in reality we do not often encounter a purely instrumentalist model of interaction between experts and decision-makers. As Rueschemeyer and Skocpol note, "social knowledge does not serve as a straightforward instrumentality of neutral bureaucrats and value-oriented politicians." (Ibid., p. 307). Various competing factions within state apparatus may use different groups of experts to justify and legitimize their respective positions on specific policies. This was the case even in the former Soviet Union and its satellites, despite apparent homogeneity of the ruling stratum and insignificant variations of opinion within academic establishment. When Gorbachev in the beginning of his reforms in 1985 appointed Aganbegian, an economist associated with Khruschev's reforms of the 1960s, his principal economic advisor, he demonstrated his commitment to moderate reforms directed to rapid improvements in economic efficiency. In 1956, Poland's new Communist leader Gomulka's decision to include Lange and Kalecki (both proponents of market elements in socialist economy) in the Council for Economic Reforms indicated a shift toward more liberal and less centralized economic policy. In both cases, the influence of new advisors on actual economic policies was very limited and short-lived (Beud and Dostaler, 1995). However, they helped to strengthen new leaders' claims to legitimacy by providing a credible negative assessment of the economic policies of their predecessors and opponents.

In a case of systemic change accompanied by a circulation of elites, the interaction between experts and decision-makers follows a pattern roughly similar to the one described above. The main difference is that, since the new rulers and their experts do not have experience of interaction that occurs in the decision-making process, their respective roles are not well determined. Before they came to power, the aspiring rulers might dominate in dialogue with their experts by imposing their vision of preferable economic models. The situation may change after the new elites gain power and have to make decisions in an unfamiliar and often unstable environment. Then the experts, who are believed to possess instrumental knowledge essential for formulation and implementation of policies, may have the upper hand in formulating economic policies.

In a "routine mode" of interaction between the rulers and the experts, the resulting decisions can be viewed as at least approximately rational. True, this rationality is, to use Simon's expression, bounded, but so is rationality in any complex organization. The bounds are imposed on rationality by specific features of information processing, organizational structure and organizational goals. Still, decision-making remains an essentially rational process as long as it is based on comparison of costs and benefits within a known and stable system of preferences. Both parties in the interaction have acquired a detailed knowledge of the system of preferences in the process of shared participation in administrative activities.

In a "transformation mode" of interaction this mutual familiarity is absent. The aspiring rulers are unable to give the experts a detailed outline of the future policies. Instead, they provide a vague image of a desirable (and often utopian) state of affairs and expect the experts to come up with a justification of this image from a "scientific" standpoint. When the detailed knowledge of the preferences of the rulers and abilities of the experts is absent, rationality of the process of policy-formation and decision-making depends on the latter's knowledge and expertise. However, the experts may have the knowledge of the old economic system, whereas their economic competence regarding the new system is likely to be scarce.

Pavel Pelikan (1993, p. 75) defines economic competence as "the competence of economic agents -- both individuals and organizations -- to receive and use information for solving economic problems and making economic decisions." The fact that in this interpretation economic competence denotes not the information but rather the ability to use it makes it close to Polanyi's "tacit knowledge" (1962) and Hayek's "dispersed information" (1967). All these notions have in common one important feature: significantly limited transferability. Thus, scarcity of economic knowledge cannot be quickly reduced and is likely to contribute to the lack of rationality in decision-making for quite some time. Even if the new rulers have positive attitudes to the capitalist market economy, transition to it is unlikely to be a rational process if the existing pool of economic experts possess scarce economic competence. In the discussion that follows I will illustrate that the Soviet tradition of economic thought created conditions of scarce economic competence regarding market economy.

The Soviet academic system, like almost every other activity in the former Soviet Union, had been of a decidedly centralized nature. Although each republic had its own Academy of Sciences, these institutions were of secondary importance. In economics and the social sciences the main academic discourse had been concentrated in Moscow and communicated to the Academies in constituent republics primarily by means of centrally published scholarly journals. Scholars from the periphery (i.e., not from Moscow) could participate in discourse by publishing their articles there. Scholarly journals published in the republics had been of lesser prestige, had not been intended for circulation outside the republic, and contained articles concerned with narrow and specific issues. Trend-setting theoretical discussions, often serving as a run-up for important policy decisions, originated almost exclusively in Moscow. Although in our analysis of the concept of the market in Soviet economic thought references will be made mostly to the centrally published economic and sociological journals, it should be noted that they reflected the discourse not only in Russia but in other Soviet republics as well. In the discussion that follows, the term "Soviet economic thought" includes economic thought in Belarus and the Baltic republics before the collapse of the Soviet Union.

Visions of Reform in Soviet Economic Thought in the Second Half of the 1980s

Generations of Soviet economists were taught to think of the market as something alien to mainstream (Soviet) economics. Problems relating to the illicit market-like activities in the centrally planned economy ("black" and "gray" markets) had been considered non-issues. Studies of the capitalist market economy existed on the periphery of the discipline of economics in a form of ideological exercises rather than positive analysis. The official title of this field of the Soviet economics -- "Political Economy and Critique of Bourgeois Economic Theories" -- implied the impossibility of any positive research on the subject. The blatantly ideological nature of the studies and lack of necessary sources due to restricted access to the books published in the West made this field of economics unattractive for many intellectually serious scholars. At the same time, methods of research developed by

Western economics were not subject to the same restrictions as Western economic theories. As Pekka Sutela points out, the optimal planning approach was considered compatible with the tenets of Marxist-Leninist ideology (Sutela, 1991). Ideological problems were avoided by declaring that while the theoretical foundations of Western economic thought remain part of a hostile ideology, practical optimization methods of Western economics are useful in the socialist planning (Sutela, 1991, p. 36). Thus, formal and highly mathematized econometric methods were quite popular among the avant-garde Soviet economists who used them mostly in research related to optimization of central planning. The situation in which methods were officially recognized as useful while their theoretical foundations were severely criticized may have contributed to the misperception of the market by the Soviet and post-Soviet reformers as merely a set of useful techniques leading to a higher economic performance.

The stagnant state of the official economic scholarship (and there was no unofficial scholarship to speak of) suited the Soviet rulers as long as they were content with performance of the economy. However, in the early 1980s the Soviet ruling elite became increasingly dissatisfied with the state of affairs. A brief campaign introduced by Andropov to strengthen discipline and improve centralized control over the economy did not achieve the desired results. By the time Gorbachev came to power the crisis state of the Soviet socio-economic system had become evident to the more far-sighted Soviet leaders.

Some authors point out that it was not the concern about the poor state of the economy per se that led the Soviet leadership to realize that drastic measures should be taken to improve the situation. Rather, it was dissatisfaction with the diminishing inputs into the development of the military system provided by the ailing economy. Laszlo Csaba notes that the first policy statements made by Gorbachev after he came to power indicated his anxiety over the possible loss of military superiority (Csaba, 1995, p. 39). Csaba goes on saying: "One can hardly exercise more sweeping -- and, with hindsight, all the more justified -- criticism of the Brezhnev years, whose main priority was subordination of all socioeconomic development to the immediate needs of the military, in order to secure an incontestable, fully-fledged superpower status, equal to that of the US."(Csaba, 1995, p. 39).

Of course, at that time the Soviet economy exhibited a whole range of shortcomings: inefficiency, waste, environmental damage, low living standards, technological backwardness, to name only a few. However, Gorbachev's reforms were not motivated by a desire to improve environmental or living standards. In the first years of Gorbachev's rule the slogan of "perestroika" (restructuring) was accompanied by "uskorenie" (acceleration). The program of accelerated economic growth was introduced in 1985. Its theoretical foundations had been laid by Abel Aganbegian, a scholar who specialized in methods of optimal planning. Instead of decentralizing control over the economy, the program of accelerated growth strengthened the power of the central ministries (Sutela, 1991, p. 147).

According to the program, accelerated growth was to be achieved by means of centralized redistribution of funds in favor of increased investments and at the expense of consumption. Structural systemic transformation of the economy directed toward decentralization of decision-making and the introduction of market-like components was not a part of the program. In fact, it called for a tightening of the central control, particularly over the implementation of centrally made decisions.

Although the program of accelerated growth did not (and could not) result in improvement of the economic performance and shared the fate of many other programs of that kind, highly publicized at the beginning then proven to be unworkable and quietly forgotten, it did have a certain impact on the development of the Soviet economic thought. Since its core theoretical elements were based on optimization techniques, certain preconditions had to be met before a formal optimization model could be created. Among the necessary prerequisites of the optimization process are: a clearly defined subject of optimization, the means to implemented the model, as well as criteria against which optimality should be measured. To define the subject and criteria of optimization, one needs to obtain a precise and detailed information about the actual and the projected state of the system. Defining the means of implementation of the model implies the question of whether the existing system of economic policy decision-making is capable of efficient implementation of the optimization model. Thus, the discussion touched two topics that had been virtually closed since the 1930s: the actual (as opposed to the officially publicized) performance of the Soviet economy and the efficiency of the vast Soviet economic bureaucracy. These two topics would dominate the Soviet scholarly discourse until the collapse of the Soviet Union.

Among attempts to come up with an adequate evaluation of the Soviet economic performance the most compelling and comprehensive was research by Grigory Khanin. In 1988 he published an article in which he argued that official statistical data on the economic growth in the Soviet Union since the 1930s had been grossly inflated and that the actual rate of growth was more modest. According to his calculations, the volume of added value in the Soviet economy in the period of 1929-87 increased 6.9 times as opposed to

89.5 times according to the official statistics. Figures for the increase in productivity for the same period were 3.55 times according to Khanin's calculations and 46.23 times according to the official statistics (Khanin, 1988).

These corrected figures of economic growth were not very damaging for the overall assessment of the Soviet economic performance. After all, the average annual 3.3 percent growth in added value is a remarkable achievement, as is 2.2 percent average annual growth in productivity. However, closer examination of Khanin's findings provided more reasons for concern. First, he maintained that economic growth was not due to increased efficiency but rather to continuing increase in use of new factors of production. The corollary was that once the limits of expansion are reached the growth will subside. Second, he indicated that these limits may have been reached by 1976-80 when average annual growth in added value dropped to 1.0 percent; in the next five year period it dropped to 0.6 percent. Corresponding figures for productivity were 0.2 percent for 1976-80 and 0.0 percent for 1981-85. These figures were especially disturbing because they indicated that not only had the limit of expansion based on new resources been reached but the system did not possess an ability to provide economic growth based on increased productivity. Although the article drew no distinction between economic expansion and economic growth, the implicit corollary was that the system had reached its limits for the former and did not have elements necessary for the latter.

The article confirmed the suspicions, long felt by the Soviet economists, that achievements of the past had been vastly exaggerated by the Party-controlled statistics and that the present economic ills cannot be remedied by yet another cosmetic reform. In view of these findings the program of accelerated growth seemed to be out of touch with reality since hardly any growth could be warranted by the existing system of government control over the economy.[3]

Some authors pointed out that centralized economic planning was not as effective as officially portrayed. The fact that five-year plans were routinely corrected as the enterprises managed to persuade planning authorities that their planned production figures were unattainable was not reflected in the official statistics. Then, plan fulfillment was routinely measured using the corrected plan figures as criteria. Medvedev and Nit (1988) questioned not only the effectiveness of the centralized planning but the adequacy of the statistical system intertwined with it.

The realization that the Soviet economy, although exhibiting high rates of growth in the past, was far from having achieved the economic miracle portrayed by official statistics and that in the last decade growth had virtually stopped led to discussion about the causes of economic stagnation. Soon the discussion focused on the oversized Soviet bureaucratic apparatus as the source of all economic ills.

The discussion did not question the fundamental principles of the Soviet economy. The dominant position of state ownership as well the leading role of the Communist Party in setting the goals of economic development were considered sacred cows. A typical argument implied that while the Party was interested in increased efficiency of the economic system as a whole and individual enterprises are in a position to increase their efficiency, a large group of bureaucrats in central planning organizations and industrial ministries was interested only in a preservation of their privileged positions and deliberately hampered the economic restructuring (e.g., Pletniov, 1988, p. 141; Popov, 1988, p. 3) pointed out that the bureaucratic apparatus was independent of the Party and has its own interests that do not necessarily lead to higher economic efficiency.

Diatribes against bureaucracy were followed by suggestions for improvement and restructuring of the economic system. The authors did not look to the Western market models for inspiration. Instead, the recipes for economic recovery were sought within the classical Marxist-Leninist tradition. It was generally accepted that the existing administrative system had been created by Stalin in the early 1930s, while the Soviet economy before that was largely free from bureaucratic distortions and close to the true teachings of Marx and Lenin.

The early writings of Marx, the late writings of Lenin, and a more profound reading of *Capital* were seriously suggested as theoretical foundations for economic restructuring. The Bolsheviks' new economic policy of the 1920s was portrayed as a system that combined reasonably high efficiency and workers' self-management within the predominantly (socialist) state property where small private and cooperative firms filled the niches left by large-scale socialist enterprises. This system of harmonious economic relations, designed by Lenin and promoted by Boukharin, fell victim to the anti-proletarian forces of bureaucracy and petty bourgeoisie thus creating a monstrous Stalinist state.[4] The real facts: that high rates of economic growth under the new economic policy were mostly due to a low starting point; that centralized bureaucratic control was much more pervasive than workers' self-management; that relations between (socialist) industry and (private) agriculture were deliberately geared in favor of the former; and finally that the whole policy was regarded by its creators as a temporary measure -- were seldom mentioned. In the mainstream of Soviet economic thought, socialist economy of the Soviet type was still perceived as a viable economic system which, if cleared of distortions and deviations of the Stalin period, could provide the necessary efficiency and sustain high rates of growth. A capitalist market economy was certainly not regarded as a desirable outcome of economic reforms.

For Soviet economists, examining economic reforms in East European socialist countries was another way to search for an efficient economic model while remaining within the socialist frame of reference. Yugoslav "market socialism" was popular among Soviet scholars. It purported to serve as living proof that socialism and a one-party political system can be combined with positive elements of the market, and this combination results in living standards much higher than in "traditional" socialist countries. Workers' self-management, which apparently was the main managerial principle in Yugoslav economy, added to its attractiveness. The writings of Yugoslav economists were frequently published in the USSR. They did not include works of authors critical of the Yugoslav economic system (e.g. Svetozar Pejovich) and concentrated mostly on the "socialist" component of market socialism, thus adding almost nothing to the reader's understanding of a market economy.

Hungary was another country whose economic reforms attracted the steady attention of Soviet economists. If in the case of Yugoslavia the focus was on workers' self-management, Hungary provided an example of a gradual loosening of the centralized controls since the reforms started in 1968[5] and of corresponding increases in efficiency and economic growth. The gradual nature of Hungarian reforms as well as the fact that they were not intended to abolish centralized control completely, but to change its methods from the direct distribution of material resources to monetary control through the banking system, appealed to most Soviet economists, still reluctant to part with the main principles of the existing economic system.

Works of Hungarian economists on various aspects of reforms were regularly published in the USSR and were well known among Soviet economic scholars. Janos Kornai was especially well-known since his books and articles started to appear in the Soviet press in the 1960s. However, his book, *The Socialist System*, published in Russian in 1990, was a revelation to many Soviet readers. The book included the ideas developed in Kornai's previous works (such as *Economics of Shortage* and *Soft Budget Constraints*) that had not been published in the USSR and were available only to a limited audience there. In these works Kornai had first proved that socialist economics has some serious inherent flaws that cannot be eliminated unless the nature of the system changes and it ceases to be socialist. Further elaborated, these ideas were presented to the Soviet reader in a clear and compelling form. For the first time a person known as a serious economist and authority on the reform process in a socialist country stated clearly and unequivocally: shortages and economic inefficiency are inherent parts of any socialist economy and cannot be eliminated by reforms. The advice to reformers was: you either live in a shortage-ridden and inefficient socialist economy and put up with it for some non-economic reason, or you should consider its transformation toward a capitalist economic system. As future events showed, Kornai's analysis of the socialist economy was closer to the real state of affairs than his scenario of market transformation. However, it was the former that was of particular importance in the Soviet Union at that time and that accounted for the impact of the book on the Soviet academic community.

Thus, it was only in 1990 that mainstream economic thought in the Soviet Union started to turn from the discussion of how to reform socialism to a realization that it cannot be reformed. The consequences were the understanding that Marxism-Leninism does not provide adequate analytical tools and that a study of capitalist markets is necessary for a meaningful analysis of economic transformation in socialist countries. However, the process of re-orientation had just started and Soviet economic thought was still influenced by traditions of its past. The economic community was unable to supply any substantial number of experts on the functioning of capitalist markets, let alone market transition, when political and economic changes started in 1991.

Soviet economists of the 1980s knew what they did not need to know and did not know what they needed to know. They knew about categories of Marxist political economy, about Lenin's plan of socialist development and Stalin's deviations from that plan, about absolute and relative impoverishment of the proletariat under capitalism, and about the dangers of exploitation posed by (even Soviet) bureaucracy. They did not know about stock exchanges and money markets, about the behavior of individual producers in different economic environments, and, surprisingly, about the role of the state in modern capitalist economies. Least of all they knew about ways of successful transition from a non-market to a market economy, the ignorance that could not be remedied by Western economic advice since no such transition had been undertaken. The years from the beginning of a relatively open discussion about the state of the Soviet economy to the avalanche of events that started with the collapse of the Soviet Union in 1991 did almost nothing to close the lacunae in the Soviet economic thought. In all the Soviet republics, market reforms were started by persons who did not have sufficient knowledge about markets and with the help of outside experts who knew even less about the specifics of market transitions in a socialist country.

The main direction of Soviet economic discourse in the late 1980s can be defined by the axis "central planning authorities -- individual enterprises". Central authorities were identified as the source of the inefficiency that stifles the initiative of individual enterprises, which legitimized the negative image of the former. This made it easier to criticize central authorities in another context: relations between the center and the periphery of the Soviet Union, especially its constituent republics.

While the main line of discourse was more concerned with economic efficiency and suggested adjustments in relations between central apparatus and enterprises in order to increase it, economic efficiency could not be easily detected in the second line of discourse. It was not obvious that centralization of decision-making process in Moscow is more detrimental to economic efficiency than would be its concentration in the hands of bureaucracies in constituent republics. Therefore, proponents of more economically independent republics pointed out that local and republican authorities are better positioned to cope with problems of environment, transport, infrastructure, urban development and public services than their counterparts in Moscow. Researchers of inter-republican trade maintained that, as a result of centralized flows of material resources, exchange between republics is not mutually beneficial, some republics receiving more net surplus than they would have under conditions of direct trade, and others suffering losses that could be avoided under a less centralized arrangement.

One beneficial consequence of this discussion was that it permitted to debate the issue of property rights without leaving the socialist frame of reference. Problems of identification of local, provincial, republican and all-Union property, as well as systems of taxation that would take these divisions into account, soon became an important part of "regionalist" economic debates. Arguments in favor of delegation of more decision-making power to the republics were supported by the local ruling elites who saw them as a justification for strengthening their positions vis-a-vis Moscow. In fact, the debates had clear political overtones, especially on such issues as property rights and the system of taxation, as well as equitable exchange in interrepublican trade.

Soon the term "republican self-financing" became as common as "self-financing of the enterprise", although the two had different connotations. If the latter meant that an enterprise should rely on its own initiative to survive and grow, the former implied that a constituent republic should receive some political powers which had hitherto been the prerogative of the central authorities.

It should be noted that these two lines of debates had different implications for the development of the market. The discussion "central authorities -- individual enterprises" included as a goal increased independence of enterprises which might be seen as a step toward a market economy. On the other hand, enterprises were not important elements in the "regionalist" line of debate. In fact, relations between enterprises and central authorities were of no importance as long as the local and republican authorities received their share of enterprises' profits. These two lines of discourse were separate in the sense that "regional independence" did not require "enterprise independence" and vice versa.

In fact, neither of the two lines of debates on the role of central authorities seriously challenged the status quo. Proponents of the "complete self-financing of enterprises" did not intend to depart from the existing system of centralized controls, but rather to make substantial modifications while preserving the fundamental principle of the system: predominantly state ownership of the factors of production. Similarly, proponents of the "self-financing of the republics" envisioned redistribution of economic power within the existing political system and did not intend to break the Union completely.

Economists and New Nationalist Politicians: A Dialogue

The second half of the 1980s was marked by the emergence and rapid development of nationalist mass movements in the constituent republics of the USSR. In the Baltic states this process became visible in the summer of 1987, when demonstrations were held in capitals of Latvia, Lithuania, and Estonia to commemorate the Baltic victims of Stalinist repressions. Later that year a similar demonstration took place in Minsk. Both in the Baltics and in Belarus the leading role in organizing these demonstrations had been played by informal groups within cultural establishment (such as Writers', Artists', Film-Makers' Unions) and academe. In the Baltics they were accompanied by human rights groups, whereas in Belarus informal associations of nationally minded youth took part in the events (Nahaylo and Swoboda, 1990, p. 281). Very soon sporadic demonstrations gave way to concerted organizational effort that culminated in the emergence of popular fronts.

Estonia led the way establishing the Estonian Popular Front in Support of Restructuring in April of 1988. Two months later a group of well-known intellectuals and cultural figures in Latvia announced the creation of the Latvian People's Front. Almost simultaneously Lithuania's Restructuring Movement (Sajudis) was created in Vilnius. In Belarus the process was more protracted. In November of 1988 abut 300 intellectuals and cultural figures announced their intention to create the Byelorussian Popular Front. However, it was not until July 1 of the next year when the inaugural congress of this movement took place.

Popular fronts were peculiar political organizations with some common features. They grew from small groups of nationally-minded intelligentsia who were aware of the crises of national cultures in their respective republics and wanted to stop the Russification seen as the main cause of these crises. Revival of the local language and culture, education of nationally-conscious citizens, study of national history figured prominently on their agendas. All these movements proclaimed their affiliation with and support for the process of restructuring (perestroika) which started under Gorbachev and their intent to help the "positive forces in the CPSU" against the "enemies of the restructuring". However, closer examination of their programs, intentions, and actions showed that these statements served only as a camouflage. Their intentions went far beyond the limited goals of the official Party policy. Each of these movements had chosen a particular event in the national history that served as the most manifest illustration of the Soviet oppression and used it to undermine legitimacy of the existing political system. For popular fronts in the Baltic states such an event was the Molotov-Ribbentropp pact of 1939 which divided Eastern Europe into Soviet and Nazi spheres of influence and paved the way for the Soviet occupation of the Baltics in 1940. In Belarus it was the discovery of mass graves dating from the late 1930s where thousands of victims of Stalin's repressions were buried. Just as the Baltic popular fronts would stage demonstrations on August 23 (the date when the Molotov-Ribbentropp pact had been signed in 1939), their Byelorussian counterparts would use the site of mass grave in Kurapaty, on the outskirts of Minsk, for their meetings.

Anti-Communism was another salient feature of the popular fronts. Although presented mostly as a rejection of the Stalinist past, it was reinforced by negative attitudes toward virtually every aspect of the economic, social, and national policies of the Communist Party. Leaders of Popular Fronts in public speeches, and in the media always equated Communist ideology with Russian imperialism.

Popular fronts emerged as mass movements with almost exclusively national and cultural agenda as well as the task of delegitimizing Communist system. However, they soon started to resemble political parties in their strategies, programs, and structures. Understanding that to attract people they had to present not only a negative image of the status quo but also produce positive suggestions on various issues of socio-economic development, the leadership of popular fronts included in their programs their views on such issues as economics, environmental protection, military reforms, etc.

Given the popular fronts' apparent inability to influence policy of the ruling elite, the visions of desirable socio-economic transformations presented in their programs were only of theoretical importance. However, the situation changed when in the spring of 1989 the nationalist opposition received its first chance to take part in the political process during the elections to the Supreme Soviet of the USSR. Then, the Baltic popular fronts' active support for their chosen candidates was crucial for their defeat of Communist contenders.[6] Lithuania was an example of an overwhelming success for the nationalist forces: Sajudis won 31 out of 39 seats allotted to the republic in the Supreme Soviet (Nahaylo and Swoboda, 1990, p. 321). But even in Belarus, where the success of the Byelorussian Popular Front (officially still *in statu nascendi* in the form of an "organizational committee") was by no means as impressive (only two nationalist candidates had been elected), the character of the nationalist opposition changed from a voluntary organization with cultural agenda to a political force capable of organizing people, articulating their demands, and mobilizing their support.

Now the original sketchy and sometimes naive views on economic problems, typical for the early programs of Popular Fronts, were not sufficient. Something more elaborate, more compelling, more suitable as a basis for practical implementation was required. Such programs could not be created by the leaders of Popular Fronts who, although well educated and even brilliant people, had very limited knowledge of economics (the leader of the Byelorussian Popular Front was an archaeologist, the leader of Sajudis a musicologist). The nationalist opposition had to find professional economists to help close the gaps in their programs.

The leadership of nationalist mass movements had certain ideas about the general outline of their economic programs: they should reflect their constituents' desire for national independence as well as opposition to the existing socialist economy. The former was more important than the latter. The "regionalist" line of economic debates drew close attention of the Popular Front leaders.

In Estonia, nationalist mass movements quickly gained support among the academic establishment. This, as well as the fact that problems of regional economic development were an important part of the officially sanctioned economic research in Estonia, helped to establish a fruitful dialogue between the economists and nationalist politicians. As early as September of 1987, the Estonian press published suggestions about turning the republic into a "self-managing economic zone" or giving the republic authority over customs control on its territory (Nahaylo and Swoboda, 1990, p. 279). These measures, well-received by the nationalist opposition, in fact were promoted by the official leadership which was interested in greater economic autonomy and tolerated at least some activities of the nationalist mass movements.[7]

Estonian economists, quite familiar with the debates on "republican self-financing", started to realize the political implications of the concept. The Estonian economist Mikhail Bronshtein, a leading authority on regional economics and a supporter of the nationalist movement, sharply criticized the centralized economic system not only for economic inefficiency but also for the harmful consequences it entailed for social and environmental aspects of life in constituent republics. He compared the central industrial ministries with transnational corporations which operate without concern for local economic, environmental, and demographic problems, as well as destroying the traditional way of life of the indigenous population. He considered "republican self-financing" not only as a means to higher economic efficiency but also as the "economic basis for political restructuring" (quoted in Nahailo and Swoboda, 1990, p. 313). Similar views were expressed by other Estonian economists, for example, A. Keerna (1988).

In Latvia, the nationalist opposition actively sought cooperation with established economic scholars. They realized that they needed not only a credible statement on economic issues in their program but also a very detailed outline of economic reforms suitable for immediate implementation. By 1989 there existed an officially approved outline of "republican self-financing" for Latvia, created by the Latvian Academy of Sciences. The Latvian Popular Front accepted the document and decided to include it in its program.

Still, they knew that the program's implementation was contingent upon the good will of the Moscow authorities. By the summer of 1989, nationalists in the Baltic states had become increasingly suspicious of Moscow's attitude toward any increased autonomy of the republics. These suspicions were reinforced by bloody confrontations between the army and nationalist demonstrators in Tbilisi in April of 1989 and, closer to home, continuous use of the inexperienced and brutal riot police against peaceful demonstrations in Riga, Vilnius, and Minsk. These suspicions were reflected in the statement issued by the Governing Board of the Latvian Popular Front, which asserted that "within the federation, which is a cornerstone of the existing concept of the republic's economic autonomy, Moscow is unlikely to cooperate honestly.

Unfortunately, the *diktat* and animosity on the part of the central authorities are increasingly felt in Latvia" (Liepa, 1989).

The leadership of Latvian Popular Front realized that the existing outline of "republican self-financing" did not provide a detailed plan of actions in a case of emergency caused by Moscow's attempts to stem the tide of national autonomy. An emergency economic program was needed. It could not be developed within the existing research institutions, still under control of the Communist Party.

The Latvian Popular Front took concrete steps to create a research group consisting of economists who understood the urgency and complexity of the situation. They recruited nine prominent Latvian economists who were told to create an economic program for a possible emergency situation (such as an economic blockade by Russia) (Liepa, 1989).

At this point, the program had nothing to do with market reforms. Entitled "The existence of independent Latvia in extreme economic conditions", it included the following issues: the structure of the minimum basic production output; the solution of the problem of energy supply; supply of material resources; food supply; a solution to the problem of potential unemployment; how to compensate for the rapid decline in living standards (*Atmoda*, July 10, 1989). The program envisioned the possibility of direct state involvement in the distribution of resources, something incompatible with the market. However, it was considered a temporary measure. The whole undertaking was of a political, rather than economic, nature. The experts were asked to come up with economic arrangements necessary for the short-term survival of Latvia should it become independent and face retaliation from Moscow. This meeting between the leadership of Latvian Popular Front and economic scholars who hitherto had not been involved in work on regional economics had one important consequence. The nationalist opposition established a dialogue with economists and created a group of economic experts independent of the official structures. This facilitated the understanding by both sides of the intricate interrelation between economic and political factors that might influence an economic reform.

Ojars Kehris, one of the economists closely collaborating with the Latvian Popular Front, draws the following distinction between regional and national economic systems: "a regional economic system, e.g. in a district, province, or republic, has mostly economic goals, whereas the national economic system has goals that are not of a strictly economic nature. The latter implies primarily the achievement of social, national, cultural goals that are related to the survival of the nation and continuity of its culture." (Kehris, 1989, p. 3). He stated that the new economic system should take into account the interests of individuals and the nation as opposed to the interests of enterprises.[8]

Nationally minded Latvian economists had a system of priorities in which the autonomy of the republic's economy occupied a higher place than market reforms. One of them, V. Vasil'ev, while criticizing the centralized economic system where decision-making is concentrated in the hands of the Union ministries, did not immediately propose a market alternative. Instead, he insisted that: "The economic system of a constituent republic should be an organizational-economic system of management that includes national and interrepublican enterprises and cooperatives. The basis of this economic system of the sovereign constituent republic should be the national property of the people of the republic, i.e. autonomous possession, use, and disposal of natural resources, means of production, manufactured goods, scientific information, and monetary resources. Procedures of possession, use, and disposal of property on behalf of the people of the republic should be determined by the republic's Supreme Soviet" (Vasil'ev, 1989, p. 11). Thus, according to this view, the first step of economic reform should be political, namely, the transferring of property rights from Moscow to the authorities of the sovereign republic. The republican legislature could then delegate these rights as it saw fit. This scenario did not exclude the possibility of market reforms, but it did not explicitly require them as the only (or even the most desirable) alternative.

The "siege mentality" of the Latvian nationalist opposition and their economic experts can be explained by the distribution of forces in Latvia prior to the collapse of the Soviet Union. Latvia had the largest share of non-indigenous population among the three Baltic states. Most non-Latvians (usually referred to as Russian-speaking population) were opposed to the idea of Latvian national independence. Their organizations were supported by the central Soviet authorities and had strong positions in large industrial enterprises. In this situation, the Latvian nationalists were afraid that Moscow could use the Russian-speaking population to disrupt the Latvian economy in order to thwart their drive for national independence. The worst-case scenario feared by the leadership of the Latvian Popular Front was an economic blockade combined with industrial strikes by non-Latvian workers. The threat was real, and preparations for an economic emergency were justified. However, they did not indicate that Latvian nationalist leaders were more hostile toward the idea of the market than their counterparts in other Baltic states or in Belarus. Cautious, yes; but certainly not hostile.

In fact, both economic blockades and a wave of strikes did affect all three Baltic states in 1990, but the damage to their economies was not as catastrophic as expected by the Latvian nationalists, nor did it lead to the drastic regulatory measures they were prepared to introduce.

Lithuania, although not entirely free from ethnic tensions, was in a somewhat better situation than its Baltic neighbors. Its Russian-speaking minority was smaller and less organized than in Latvia and was not concentrated in one region as in Estonia. In fact the Polish minority, concentrated in the Vilnius region (although not in Vilnius itself), provided greater reason for concern than the dispersed and not so well organized Russian-speaking population.

Of course, the problems of the Polish minority were unlikely to cause a political and economic emergency.[9] This situation was reflected in a dialogue between the Sajudis leadership and economic experts. The former did not ask the latter to create a plan of action for a possible economic blockade imposed by Moscow and industrial strikes by the Russian-speaking workers. However, as with their colleagues in Latvia, Lithuanian economists were asked by Sajudis to use economic methods to achieve political ends.

In 1988 Sajudis published a draft program in which a desirable economic system was supposed to have all natural resources (including land) and means of production as the property of the independent Lithuanian state. As to other economic reforms, they were confined to the "economic autonomy" of enterprises without further elaboration (*Sajudzio Zinios*, December 6, 1988). This attitude was similar to that of the Latvian Popular front and its economic experts: political measures to transfer property rights from Moscow to the republic are more urgent and important than market reforms, which can be worked out later.

Sajudis from the beginning attracted some well-established Lithuanian economists. The most prominent figure among them was Kazimera Prunskene, who was in fact a founding member of Sajudis. In 1989 she became a Deputy Prime Minister of the Lithuanian SSR. The fact that a person very closely associated with the nationalist movement could be promoted to one of the highest positions in the republic's administrative apparatus is in itself an indication of the tolerance with which the Lithuanian (at that time still Communist) authorities treated the nationalist opposition.

Two elements were salient in the writings of Lithuanian economists: first, they insisted that devolution would increase the economic efficiency of the decision-making process in the Soviet Union in general, and second, they pointed out that the republics' rights to control economic assets on their territories were non-economic in nature. The first statement appealed to "instrumental rationality" by promising better economic performance for the whole Soviet system, whereas the second had more far-reaching implications:

it asserted that republics have certain rights that are inherent rather than conferred on them by Moscow.

For example, Prunskene wrote that "economic autonomy of the republics is a necessary condition for efficient restructuring of control over the Soviet economy as a whole" (Prunskene, 1989, p. 3). However, in the same article she stated that: "economic development of any republic should be based on the principle of regionalism, i.e. on *centuries-old traditions of economic thinking and motivations of a particular nation.* The right of republics to autonomously control their economies is just as *natural* as the right of a nation or a person to exist. The fact that the rights are absent in the economic sphere (as well as elsewhere) is the largest and most urgent problem" (Prunskene, 1989, pp. 3-4, italics added).

In the above statements, as in works of many other economists from the Baltic states, there is a clear distinction between economic efficiency as a purely instrumental category and the nation's right to autonomous economic development regarded as the cornerstone of economic restructuring. In this particular article economic efficiency might seem to be presented as an end, with decentralization of the decision-making process merely a means toward this end. However, the author asserted that not every method of economic decentralization is equally efficient. Delegation of decision-making rights to enterprises in her view was not as efficient as devolution of economic controls to republics.

Another important point: the goal of increased efficiency was emphasized only in the context of the Soviet Union and seldom mentioned in discussion of economic arrangements within republics. There, attention was concentrated on the issues of property rights of republics as well as their preservation as economic, cultural and territorial entities. The article appeared in *Voprosy Ekonomiki* (*Problems of Economics*), the leading Soviet economic journal, and was therefore addressed to the audience outside the Baltic states. Thus, it is fair to assume that the promise of higher economic performance if a Union is less centralized was intended to justify the increasing independence of republics. Then the latter, rather than the former, becomes the real goal.

In Belarus, relations between the nationalist opposition (Byelorussian Popular Front) and the official economic scholarship were very different from those in the Baltics. The economists belonging to the academic establishment were reluctant to collaborate with nationalist mass movements and to accept the legitimacy of national independence as the main goal. If in the Baltics the notion of the property rights of the republics was common both in documents of the nationalist movements and in the writings of local economists, in

Belarus there was a visible difference between the two. The first version of the economic program of the Byelorussian Popular Front included the clause about property rights of the republic on all assets located on its territory (very similar to the programs of the Baltic nationalists) (*Naviny BNF*, December 1988). At the same time, documents of the official research institutions did not even mention republican property as a desirable outcome of reforms.

Belarus had a unique position in the territorial division of labor in the former Soviet Union. It was the only constituent republic which coincided with the "economic region", the territorial unit used for planning purposes. This position contributed to the existence of a salient "regional" direction of the local economic research. Even before the Gorbachev reforms, Belarus frequently participated in economic experiments designed to improve efficiency of the regional economy. Thus, Byelorussian economists were thoroughly familiar with the regional aspects of economic restructuring and contributed a great deal to this line of economic discourse in the late 1980s.

The official Byelorussian research on regional economic problems was built on the premise that the preservation of the political status quo in the Soviet Union, and the optimization of inputs of each region into the all-Union growth of economic efficiency was central. A draft decree on the introduction of the republican self-financing in Belarus prepared by the research institute of the Byelorussian Planning Committee envisioned the principal tasks of territorial self-financing as: the planned and proportional development of the socialist production on the basis of mutual coordination of all branches and enterprises of national economy; the rational distribution, utilization, and reproduction of local raw materials; regional division of labor and development of inter-branch production facilities; utilization of underutilized production facilities and equipment; development of infrastructure to be used by all regional industrial enterprises; rationalization of inter-branch and inter-regional economic relations ("On the transition of BSSR to economic conditions of territorial self-financing" Draft Decree of the Council of Ministers of the USSR, Byelorussian Planning Committee, 1988). In this document, the republic is a mere territorial entity, a space where enterprises, deposits of raw materials, and infrastructure are located and can be disposed in the interest of increased efficiency.

A similar document prepared by the Economic Research Institute of the Byelorussian Academy of Sciences was not different in its attitude toward the republic as a means to improve the economy of the Soviet Union as a whole. In fact, it suggested that the republic was not the most suitable unit of territorial planning and proposed that the province (oblast) should be the principal unit of the territorial self-financing ("On the transition of BSSR to economic conditions of territorial self-financing" Draft Decree of the Council of Ministers of the USSR, Byelorussian Academy of Sciences, 1988). Thus, even a remote political implication of that the republic should be granted a modicum of economic autonomy was avoided. Both documents envisioned the redistribution of financial resources between the enterprises on the one hand and local and republican authorities on the other hand in favor of the latter. However, the local and republican governments had no right to levy taxes; redistribution was to proceed according to rates established by the central authorities in Moscow. This was a far cry from the contemporary writings of the Baltic economists who considered a devolution of political power to the republics the main goal of economic restructuring.

Byelorussian economists continued to adhere to the premise of the centralized Soviet political system as late as 1991, just months before the collapse of the Soviet Union. Mikhail Nikitenko and Gennady Lych, two leading Byelorussian experts on regional economic development, wrote: "A constructive approach to the problem of [republican] sovereignty lies in a method of creating a system of controls over the regional economy in which neither autonomy or sovereignty of the region, nor regional property rights, constitute the main premise. On the contrary, the sphere of economic relations and the choice of a rational method for their realization in a particular conditions, are the most important. Only then should these relations and economic mechanism for their realization be given a corresponding form of sovereignty and property rights" (Lych and Nikitenko, 1991, p. 133). Note that the authors do not mention the word "republic", using "region" instead as the politically more neutral term. The underlying premise was clear: the republic was not regarded as a political entity, but rather as a territorial unit that should serve as a vehicle to facilitate higher economic performance.

The nationalist opposition tried to change the outlook of the Byelorussian economists starting in 1988. After all, it needed expert advice, not only for immediate practical purposes (the BPF did not reach the point when it could consider its ascent to power a real possibility until 1990), but, more importantly, to give a greater credibility to the economic program in the eyes of the general public. Several times leaders of the BPF approached prominent Byelorussian economists and asked for their help in work on the economic part of their program. However, their attempts were futile. In the Baltic states members of the official economic establishment were routinely present in all important events organized by the nationalist movements, such as congresses, leadership meetings, and the joint meetings of the Baltic nationalists (Baltic Assemblies). In Belarus, not only did directors of the leading economic research institutions not attend nationalist meetings, but they expressly forbade their subordinates to do so. The Byelorussian academic establishment successfully distanced itself from the nationalist movement, thus precluding a possibility of a fruitful dialogue.

The following four entities, reflected in the academic debates on economic reform, were present in economic programs of nationalist mass movements in the Baltics and in Belarus: individual, enterprise (workers' collective), administrative system (mostly, the all-Union industrial ministry), constituent republic (region). The individual, while only of peripheral importance in the mainstream economic discourse, occupied a central position in programs of all Popular Fronts.

In the economic program of the Estonian Popular Front the individual is mentioned frequently in two economic roles: as owner and as consumer. The opening statement of the program maintains that decentralization of economic decision-making and the development of an economy with diverse system of property rights will revive a "laborer-owner and satisfied consumer" (Economic Program of the EPF, 1990). Development of "economic democracy" is seen as a means to create conditions for the emergence of individual owners. The Estonian program was the only one to mention private property as a desirable arrangement and to state that "private property of the means of production cannot and should not be a temporary economic measure, but should have constitutional guaranties" (*Ibid.*). Special attention is paid to the emergence of individual farmers, a process regarded as highly desirable and deserving state support. Two other statements regarding individual included consumer protection and desirability of an economic system geared toward consumer.

In the economic program of the Lithuanian Sajudis the place of the individual in the proposed economic system is treated rather vaguely. It states that the economic system of Lithuania should be restructured so as to serve the individual, that individuals "should be returned the right to independently control production and profit" (Economic Program of Sajudis, 1990). The program stated that individuals in rural areas should be given the right to become farmers and that they should enjoy the state protection. The issue of property rights was not as clear-cut as in the Estonian program. The program did not mention private property, however, it considered individual property (including that of the means of production) a desirable element in the overall system of diverse property rights and proclaimed its constitutional protection as an essential right. Describing agricultural development, the program mentioned "farmers-landowners" (*Ibid.*). A special clause of the program stated the movement's opposition to social inequality, oppression and exploitation.

While the economic programs of the nationalist movements in the Baltic states envisioned the individual as a primary actor in the economic sphere, and a person's rights to own property as the chief principle of the new economic system, their Byelorussian counterparts were much more restrained in their views regarding the place of the individual in economic system. The economic sections of the program of the Byelorussian Popular Front hardly mentioned the individual at all. Agriculture was the only activity where the program visualized a private person as an economic actor, not owning land, however, but rather permitted to use it under conditions of long-term lease. The notion of private property was completely absent and individual property barely mentioned. In the program the individual was discussed under the heading of "Social Justice" where she was perceived as a passive recipient of goods and services, while the state apparatus was to ensure the just and equitable distribution.

The enterprise (workers' collective) found a mixed reflection in nationalist economic programs. The Estonian program called for autonomous decision-making by industrial enterprises and for the transfer of state enterprises to the control of workers' collectives. At the same time, it stated that the state-owned enterprises should have more independence in their economic activities. Seen mostly in a negative light, enterprises were also regarded as posing a potential threat of undesirable demographic changes. The Estonian economic program stated that "the Popular Front is opposed to the importation of workers into Estonia" and called for enterprises to make public their plans regarding expansion of the workforce.

The Latvian and Lithuanian nationalist movements also expressed their concerns about the increased migration from other republics caused by the expansion of industrial enterprises. The economic program of Sajudis stated that "the Movement supports economic, legal, and administrative measures to regulate the demographic system (sic) and to protect the interests of the local population against the arbitrary actions of enterprises that bring people from other republics, thus complicating the supply of goods and services" (Economic Program of Sajudis, 1990).

The enterprise in its Soviet form was not regarded positively by the Baltic nationalists. Sajudis stated in its program that "The Movement supports only those enterprises that are built on democratic, voluntary principles and do not have extensive administrative apparatus" -- a thinly veiled criticism of the existing industrial enterprises that were the opposite of the ideal that Sajudis would support. To Latvians, Lithuanians, and Estonians the existing industrial enterprises were unwieldy, polluting, obsolete and inefficient entities whose impact on the life of the local communities and the nation in general was decidedly negative. Of course, in a dichotomy "enterprise -- all-Union authorities" the nationalist would prefer enterprises since they, at least theoretically, could be restructured.

The economic program of the Byelorussian nationalist movement had a somewhat different view on the role of the enterprise in the restructured economy. The program stated that "The central link of the economic system should be the independent enterprise that operates according to principles of self-government and self-financing" (Program of the Byelorussian Popular Front, 1990). The workers' collective was supposed to determine the form of property of the enterprise. The program stated that collective property in the means of production should be predominant in the Byelorussian economy and insisted that workers' collectives should be given the right to "independently dispose of the products of their labor". By "independent" enterprise the authors of the program meant that it should not be subject to direct planning and control by the central administrative system.

The latter, however, found very detailed reflection in Byelorussian program, according to which: "general management of the economy of Belarus should be conducted by its ministries and state committees". This statement was followed by eleven functions that the authors of the program considered desirable for the administrative system, which ought, among other things, to "determine policy of research and technological development", "determine investment priorities and distribute subsidies to stimulate growth of the key branches of economy", "stabilize the market", "facilitate decrease of prices", "facilitate optimal territorial allocation of production forces", etc. To perform these functions, the administrative system was supposed to use subsidies, state orders, credit incentives. Thus, the administrative vision of the Byelorussian nationalists was very far from a market model.

In the program of the Lithuanian nationalists, the administrative system was not presented in such detail. However, its main functions were envisioned as the distribution of subsidies, price control, the creation of research programs and technological development. As did the Byelorussian program, it deliberately included elements alien to the ideal type of market in the list of desirable government activities. By contrast, the Estonian program did not mention any particular role of the administrative system in the future economy of independent Estonia. The only reference to the administrative system was a negative one: its destruction was presented as a major precondition for the success of the reforms.

The idea of the republic as a political, cultural and ecological entity was salient in each of the four programs. The Estonian program stated that "the interests of our republic are best served by its transition to full self-financing, for which the political sovereignty of the Estonian SSR is an indispensable precondition as well as a constituent part". In the Lithuanian program the economic autonomy of republics was considered an indispensable element of their sovereignty. The programs of all three Baltic nationalist movements were committed to introducing their own national currencies as a means of supporting the economic autonomy of the republics.

The economic program of the Byelorussian nationalist opposition was, surprisingly, not so straightforward about the place of the republic in the projected economic order. It declared that the republic's economic autonomy should be based on the division of labor within the Soviet Union, hardly a statement one would expect from a movement whose main goal supposedly was national independence. Interestingly enough, the program also envisioned the Byelorussian economy as "harmoniously integrated into the European economic structure". How the republic's position within the all-Union division of labor would influence this "harmonious integration", remained one of the many questions which the authors of the program decided to leave unanswered. In fact, the republic was treated as a set of administrative institutions rather than as a clearly defined political entity.

In the economic programs of the three Baltic Popular Fronts national independence was clearly presented as the main goal, while economic reforms were only part of the overall program to achieve this goal. The Byelorussian nationalist opposition presented a somewhat more cautious view. There were other differences, particularly regarding the positions of various economic actors in the projected economic system. However, the main feature was similar among all four programs: none of them exhibited a clear and unequivocal commitment to a market economy. The main precondition for a market economy, a system of property rights where private property occupies a central place, was treated with particular caution by nationalist parties in the Baltic states as well as in Belarus. The predominant attitude among the nationalist politicians seemed to be: "let's establish control over the republic's economy first and think about specifics later."

The Case of Poland: An Unlikely Prelude to Market Transformation

Polish economists were not so remote from mainstream Western economic thought as their Soviet colleagues. In fact, such Polish scholars as Oscar Lange and Michal Kalecki had made significant contribution to the development of economic thought in the West as well as in Poland. Both economists started to advocate an alternative to the laissez-faire capitalism in the 1930s, when criticism of the self-regulating free markets was *en vogue* in Western universities. Asserting that socialism is theoretically feasible, Lange attempted to prove that a centrally controlled economy does not have to be inefficient. He proposed a model of economy, based on the state ownership of the means of production, that would combine individual economic incentives with centralized macroeconomic regulation. The model included two sets of prices: one determined by supply and demand (on most consumer goods) and another, so-called "accounting prices", established by the central planning authority (for the means of production). This model, that implied a coexistence of state-owned and private economic entities in a socialist economy, became widely known as "market socialism". Lange pursued this line of research since the 1930s well into the 1960s and not only influenced the course of economic thought in the socialist countries but also provided arguments to many Western advocates of a more direct state involvement in economic processes.

Kalecki came up with an essentially Keynesian model of macroeconomic processes (with particular emphasis on business cycle) at approximately the same time as (and to a large extent independently of) Keynes himself. His influence on Keynes's disciples, particularly Joan Robinson and Nicholas Kaldor, placed him among the founders of post-Keynesian school of economic thought (Beaud and Dostaler, 1995). In 1955 Kalecki returned to Poland where he conducted research on economic growth, trying to reconcile his vision of a decentralized democratic socialist economy with a Keynesian frame of reference (although he never hesitated to criticize Keynes for the latter's belief in the viability of capitalism).

The works of Lange and Kalecki, for obvious reasons considered legitimate by the Communist establishment, provided mainstream Polish economic thought with a respectable intellectual tradition. Unlike their Soviet counterparts, who had to rely on flimsy ideological constructs, the official Polish economists could claim a solid theoretical foundation for their studies, a reasonably sophisticated paradigm that did not contradict ideological cognitive models of the old "political masters".

Of course, we are more interested in the new elites that had been brought to power by the decade-long dissent, in which Solidarity and the intellectuals associated with it played a crucial role. Since Solidarity was a free trade union that consisted mostly of blue-collar workers, one can hardly expect it to be committed to a market economy. In fact, the economic thinking of the Solidarity leadership centered around the immediate improvement of the workers' material conditions, without much thought as to how this improvement might be achieved.[10]

It is interesting to note that Solidarity, from the time it emerged on the Polish political scene, came to symbolize a force capable of directing positive changes in society and dealing with broad social issues, of a material as well as a moral nature. Wlodzimierz Suleja reflects on this attitude that became a part of the Polish political mythology when he writes that for the general public Solidarity represented "the solidarity of people deprived of their rights and freedoms and put into position of inanimate objects (*przedmiotovej roli*), people who now have awakened and are fighting for their self-determination" (Suleja, 1994, p. 229). The notion of self-determination, as well as related notions of self-government and self-organization, is especially important since it was a central element of discourse within Solidarity circles. These three notions were used to describe desirable social, political, and economic arrangements and denoted something close to the concept of civil society: a plurality of voluntary associations independent of the government. The intellectuals affiliated with Solidarity had built their ideas about desirable economic transformations around self-organized and self-governing collectivities.

The most important group of Polish dissident intellectuals affiliated with Solidarity was the Workers' Defense Committee (better known by its Polish acronym, KOR). KOR had been established in 1976 and worked closely with Solidarity since its emergence in 1980. Its members, including Jacek Kuron, Jan Lipski, Adam Michnik, and Tadeusz Mazoviecki, served as political and economic advisors to the Solidarity leadership.   The idea of self-determination and self-government as a means of political and economic change in Poland was introduced by Kuron and generally supported by other prominent KOR members. Eventually it had found its way into the Solidarity program. A self-governing territorial group was considered the main agent of political process (on the local level), independent (self-governing) institutions were envisioned as elements of the future political system in Poland, while the main element of the economic system was self-managing workers' collective (Zuzowski, 1992, p. 200).

Even though one could conceivably imagine a free market at least theoretically compatible with the idea of workers' self-management, the KOR members never regarded an essentially market capitalist economy as a desirable economic arrangement. In fact, most of them opted for an essentially state-controlled economy. Zuzowski (1992, p. 117) quotes Kuron's statement that under democratic rule the control of the national economy can be exercised through a multiparty system. Neither KOR nor Solidarity were in favor of privatization of large state-owned enterprises, but envisioned a system of protection for workers' rights in the setting of state-owned enterprises (Lipski, 1985, p. 339). It is ironic that it was Tadeusz Mazowiecki, one of the most prominent members of KOR, who presided over the ambitious Polish privatization program during his tenure as a prime-minister.

In the 1980s, the official Polish economic discourse focussed on the problem of relations between the enterprise and the central authorities. This direction was typical for a late Communist reform economy and so were the limits of discourse. On one end of the intellectual and ideological spectrum were proponents of a more traditional Soviet-type economy in which central planning authorities and branch ministries were supposed to keep their dominant position. For example, Sadowski (1987) argued that "central administrative apparatus should retain an important role in economy and cannot further reduce its existing power".

The opposite side of the spectrum was occupied by the proponents of a moderate decentralization. Arguing along the lines of Lange's model of market socialist economy, they pointed to the inability of the central planning authorities to adequately evaluate all aspects of both macro- and microeconomic processes and advocated the need to confine government economic activities to the macroeconomic regulation. According to Pajestka (1987), everyday activities of the enterprises should be controlled by management and workers, investment decisions remaining a prerogative of central authorities.

The limits of the official economic discourse in Poland in the 1980s were set by ideological framework of the Communist society. Two issues were excluded from the discussion: the domination of the Communist Party and public (in reality, state) ownership of the means of production. Thus, the official economic establishment could only discuss the means to improve performance of the existing economic system. The possibility of systemic change could not be openly discussed within the existing system of intellectual and ideological constraints.

Unlike the Soviet Union, in Poland there was an alternative economic discourse. Unlike Hungary, it remained unofficial until the collapse of the Communist regime. Throughout the 1980s it was not associated with any political opposition, remaining an intellectual exercise rather than an economic policy advice.

Leszek Balcerowicz, then a young scholar at the Central School of Economics and Statistics in Warsaw, together with a small group of colleagues, initiated a decade of informal work on various scenarios of economic reforms. His work was a radical departure from the dominant frame of reference. He envisioned the transition for a capitalist market by means of changing property rights and a series of macroeconomic monetary measures. Approximately at the same time, Janusz Lewandowski started to work on a detailed privatization program that would transfer property rights from the state to the public, thus creating a "society of capitalists".

For several years, the works of Balcerowicz and Lewandowski remained largely unknown outside their professional circle.[11] There was no dialogue between neo-liberal economists and the leaders of political opposition. Meanwhile, economic reforms in Poland were conducted by the Communist regime and according to blueprints provided by the official economic establishment. As we shall see in the next chapter, these reforms played not an insignificant role in the changing of economic views of Solidarity.

Images of the Future Economic Systems: A Summary and Comparison

In all five countries of our sample the aspiring new elites (nationalist opposition in the four Soviet republics and Solidarity in Poland) did not regard economic efficiency as a crucial feature of the desirable new economic system. In fact, the official Soviet economists were much more concerned with ways to improve economic performance.

Neither nationalists in the Baltics and Belarus nor Polish dissident intellectuals and Solidarity leaders had economic transformations high on their lists of priorities. The former were preoccupied with national independence, the latter with workers' rights and material conditions as well as the creation of civil society. Their economic programs were geared to the achievement of those primary goals.

Most importantly, there was no significant variation in attitude toward market economy among the aspiring elites in the Baltics and Poland. None of them exhibited a strong and unequivocal commitment to market transition. In fact, all of them viewed the market with some apprehension as a system built on unfettered individual pursuit of material ends and therefore potentially dangerous to the models of desirable social systems that placed the collectivity in a central position.

There is no variation of centrality of market in scholarly discourse. Due to the lack of familiarity with actual market processes and constrained by dominant intellectual traditions as well as ideological dogmas, official scholarship was unable and unwilling to come up with a credible model of market arrangements. Those experts who worked with the opposition did not represent a market-oriented direction of economic thought. In Poland, they promoted their own ideas of a non-market economy. In the Baltic states and Belarus they were asked to provide economic justification for national independence rather than create a viable market model.

Thus, the cross-national variations in the speed of market transformation could not be plausibly attributed to differences in economic knowledge and commitment to market economy among the new elites and their experts.

Notes

1   Focussing on the role of ruling elites (both old and new) and intellectuals does not mean that other social groups are ignored. However, in the discussed time period most of the new social classes and groups were *in statu nascendi* and thus not sufficiently organized to play a major role in the conduct of economic reforms. Some previously existing groups did influence economic transition policies. Among them were industrial workers whose organizational pattern was based on large state-owned industrial enterprises. Together with management, they had significant impact on some aspects of reform policies, particularly the process of privatization. Their role will be discussed in Chapters Three and Four.

2   The time factor has a special importance in this process. As Keynes observed, social and economic theories affect decision-makers "not, indeed, immediately, but after a certain interval; for in the field of economic and political philosophy there are not many who are influenced by new theories after they are twenty-five or thirty years of age, so that the ideas which civil servants and politicians and even agitators apply to current events are not likely to be the newest." (Keynes, 1936 [1964], pp. 383-384).

3   In fact, while the program of accelerated growth envisioned increased investments, Khanin pointed out that significant new investments are useless in the economy where the existing equipment is constantly under-utilized. Instead, he insisted on increased efficiency of investments, a concept alien to the traditional Soviet theory of economic growth.

4   "Bureaucratic distortion of the Soviet power was a fertile soil for bureaucratic arbitrariness: an illiterate and economically dispersed peasant mass as well as bourgeois influence on the apparatus of proletarian dictatorship and the Communist Party. It created conditions for the shift of political power from the working class to the upper levels of economic bureaucracy" (Kolganov and Buzgalin, 1988, p. 27).

5   The fact that Hungarian economic reforms started even earlier as a direct response of the ruling elite's insecurity caused by the popular uprising of 1956 was not highly publicized in the Soviet economic literature for obvious reasons.

6   Candidates supported by Popular fronts were not necessarily their members. In some cases they belonged to the establishment. In Latvia, for example, the Popular Front in one electoral district supported a Secretary of the Central Committee of Latvian Communist Party, in another district -- a Deputy Prime Minister (*Atmoda*, April 17, 1989).

7   Nahaylo and Swoboda (1990, p. 297) write that the Estonian People's Front had been organized by reformist and nationally-minded Communist intellectuals.

8   This dichotomy (individual and the nation versus the enterprise) will be better understood if we recall that in Latvia (as well as in other Baltic states) large industrial enterprises employed large numbers of people who migrated from other Soviet republics after the war.

9   According to some Lithuanian researchers, the Polish minority in Lithuania was not homogeneous, but consisted of several ethnically distinctive groups united only by a common language. Their consolidation was considered a positive process (V. Chekmonas, 1989).

10   "During most of the 1980-1981 period Solidarity refused to develop a comprehensive economic program, probably to avoid being drawn into a hopeless argument. Only in 1981

did Solidarity come out in favor of a reform program based on worker self-management, but largely because of its political features." (Slay. 1994. p. 52).

11   It was not until 1988 that Lewandowski published the first version of his privatization program. Balcerowicz's economic views first became known to the general public in 1989. when he became a deputy prime minister in charge of economic reforms.

3 Conditions and Outcomes of the First Stage of post-Soviet Economic Reforms

When leaders of the nationalist opposition movements in the former Soviet Union, or Solidarity leaders and intellectuals in Poland, were preparing drafts of their economic programs, they did not foresee the rapidity of the collapse of the Soviet-dominated political and economic system. In fact, their programs were built on a tacit assumption that their countries would remain within a well-defined Soviet sphere of influence for a considerable time. The main points of their economic programs could have been realized only under conditions of continuing cooperation with Russia and other Soviet republics. For Poland, COMECON provided the important framework for a semblance of economic normalcy, if not well-being, that allowed the Solidarity intellectuals to picture the state-controlled industrial enterprise as a major element of the desirable socio-economic order. In the Baltics and Belarus, the nationalist opposition leaders envisioned an economic system less dependent on Moscow and with some liberalization of private economic activities, but still with the central redistributive role of the state. However, when they came to power, opposition leaders in the Baltics and Poland had to face a reality quite different from what they anticipated. This reality provided a set of choices that they had not been prepared to make during their opposition years. In Belarus, the old elites which retained power after the republic became independent were equally unprepared for the new economic conditions thrust upon them by the dissolution of the Soviet Union. In all five countries decision-makers had to face economic challenges of essentially the same nature. Their responses, however, varied significantly.

Market Reforms in Poland: Economic Neo-Liberalism and Anti-Communism

Contrasting economic neo-liberalism with anti-Communism might seem implausible. The latter is an ideology, while the former is a set of theoretical postulates that in the context of post-Communist socio-economic transformations is frequently used as a foundation for market reform policy. However, as the discussion below will illustrate, particular policies of the Polish Communist government in the 1980s together with the delegitimation of the Communist regime and the growing anti-Communist sentiment contributed to the emerging perception of the neo-liberal model of market reforms as the only viable economic policy. To understand why the actual economic policy of the first non-Communist Polish government was so different from the original economic programs adopted by the opposition in the early 1980s, we must first examine the economic reforms conducted by a succession of Communist governments during the 1980s.

Until the final collapse of the Soviet bloc, external economic conditions for Poland (as well as other East European countries) were set mostly by the COMECON (Council for Mutual Economic Assistance). This organization not only coordinated and directed foreign trade of its participants, it influenced every aspect of development and international division of labor in East European economies. There are conflicting accounts of the COMECON performance. When viewed from a purely economic standpoint, its assessment is almost universally negative. Slay (1994) points out the isolation of the COMECON members from Western sources of capital, technology, consumer goods, and managerial know-how. According to Brada (1992), significant differences in economic endowments of individual members led to an inefficient trade system where importers had to buy goods from high-cost suppliers within the bloc instead of turning to low-cost producers from outside the organization. Holzman (1976) summed up the views of most Western observers by asserting that "it is safe to infer that COMECON is a losing proposition in economic terms".

Another direction of research concentrated on economic gains and losses of individual COMECON members. The debate started as early as 1950s, shortly after the emergence of the COMECON. Since the USSR was the principal force behind the process of East European economic integration, some observers regarded the Soviet economy as the beneficiary of the intra-bloc trade at the expense of other COMECON members. In one of the first detailed studies of the intra-COMECON trade, Menderhausen (1959, 1960) discovered that the Soviet Union paid its East European partners for their manufactured goods on average 15% less than to Western exporters of similar goods. This led him to conclude that the Soviet Union exploits its trade partners in the bloc. This view was challenged by Holzman (1965), who found that the overall price structure in COMECON trade was not detrimental to any of its members and the trade was mutually beneficial. More recently, studies by Marrese and Vanous (1983) showed that it was the Soviet Union that was exploited by other members of the bloc. According to this research, the Soviet Union was implicitly subsidizing its partners by selling to them raw materials and fuel at prices lower than could be obtained on world markets while paying world market prices for low-quality East European manufactured goods.

Some authors, although acknowledging the existence of the price disparity between raw materials and manufactured goods, disagreed with claims that it benefitted East European economies. Koeves (1983) argued that it was this disparity that perpetuated an obsolete production structure in Eastern Europe, eliminated incentives for improvement and innovation, and isolated the COMECON countries from the world economy.

As virtually all researchers seem to agree, economically, the COMECON was neither a system serving to increase efficiency, nor a mechanism of net wealth redistribution for the benefit of some members at the expense of others. However, if we consider the political aspect of the organization, the view of the COMECON as a reasonably effective means toward specific political ends would be quite plausible. True, the reliance of East European economies on the Soviet Union caused technological stagnation. However, up to a certain point, the Soviet economy was ready to tolerate low quality and relative technological backwardness of East European imports, especially since their quality often exceeded that of similar goods made by Soviet producers. At the same time, economic suboptimality of the COMECON arrangements served important political purposes. First, it reinforced political and ideological loyalty among the members, since the isolation from Western markets meant that any attempt by a satellite state to leave the sphere of Soviet domination would lead to economic ruin. Second, Soviet-type economic structure in each satellite country, together with intra-COMECON division of labor, made it easier for the local Communist rulers to maintain social and political stability.

Polish economy provides a good example of how investment policies based on the COMECON trade pattern influenced political situation in the country. Post-war Polish industrialization was of the Soviet type: with investments concentrated in heavy industries at the expense of agriculture and consumer goods production. While in 1955 42.3% of net material product were produced by agriculture and 37.2%, by industry and construction, by 1970 the figures were 22.7% and 55.7% respectively (Slay, 1994, p.31). Most post-war investment projects created large industrial enterprises that often employed tens of thousands of workers. These enterprises were too large for the Polish market and lacked competitiveness necessary for successful export to the West. However, the administratively determined demand for their products in the USSR and, to a lesser extent, in other COMECON countries was guaranteed. Such giants of the Polish industry as steel plants in Katowice, textile factories in Lodz (founded at the turn of the century and modernized after World War Two), and shipyards in Gdansk worked almost exclusively for the Soviet market. Unlike Hungary, Poland relied more completely on heavy, labor- and capital-intensive industries. Unlike Czechoslovakia, Polish heavy industries were created "from scratch" in the post-war years and based on the imported Soviet technology. This industrial structure was conducive to political arrangements where politicized economy and "economized polity" (Bunce, 1992, p. 27) together served to reinforce the Communist regime.

Large enterprises with relatively low technology and simple product mix well corresponded with the Soviet-type system of centralized planning and control. From the purely economic standpoint, the initial rationale for the large enterprises was economy of scale. However, this economy was offset by the fact that these enterprises often were negative added value producers (Kulig and Lipowski, 1994, p. 24). Political and administrative control over the economy was more important for the Communist leaders than narrowly defined economic efficiency.

The ability of the COMECON economy to absorb large quantities of low-quality high-cost goods served as an economic foundation of the social compact between the Communist rulers and the general population. This social compact was an important element of the late Communist political systems. Communist leaders provided economic security, tolerated low discipline and inefficiency. In return they expected political compliance from the general public. While the social compact existed in one form or another in every country of the Soviet bloc, for East European countries and Poland in particular it had special importance since the legitimacy of the Communist regime there was rapidly weakening. The economic foundations acquired additional importance, and the COMECON trade mechanism was actively used to reinforce them. Bunce (1992) suggests that the Soviet rulers deliberately forced the economy to perform the function of political integration within the bloc.

COMECON's detrimental consequences for the Polish economy became apparent when Poland's attempts to modernize its industry by importing Western investment goods and boost its living standards by increased imports of Western foodstuffs and consumer goods resulted in a severe economic crisis. In the 1970s Polish government adopted a strategy of import-led economic expansion. Western imports were paid for by Western loans which in turn were supposed to be serviced and eventually repaid by proceeds from exports to the West of the goods produced with the use of imported technology. However, imported industrial equipment was administratively distributed among the existing state-controlled enterprises. The latter lacked the incentives to use the new technologies efficiently. Consequently, the planned increase in export potential of the Polish economy failed to materialize. In 1980 Poland's ratio of debt-service payments to the hard-currency exports was 83.2% (Slay, 1994, p. 45). By the end of the 1970s Poland was left with large foreign debt and the economy structurally unable to meet its foreign financial obligations and maintain acceptable living standards at the same time.

The economic crisis of the late 1970s and early 1980s was exacerbated by the rise of the opposition to the regime, numerous strikes that paralyzed the economy, and the emergence of Solidarity as a viable political power. Communist regime in Poland faced a threat that required immediate and urgent action.

Polish Communist rulers encountered similar politico-economic crises before. In 1956, as in 1970, the sequence of events was similar to that in 1980. Exacerbation of economic problems, reflected in sharp decline of living standards, precipitated political unrest among industrial workers. The PUWP (Polish United Workers' Party) counteracted with promises of economic reforms and the removal of the old Party leadership. After first steps of economic reforms were implemented, the unrest subsided and the regime gradually slipped back to its usual policies that in several years would produce another crisis.

In the Polish practice of crisis resolution, economic reforms were used to protect the PUWP's monopoly on political power from the immediate threat posed by workers' collective actions. In the words of Jadwiga Staniczkis (1992), these reforms were "systemic shock absorbers". Twice, in 1956 and in 1970, economic reforms did absorb the political shock. It is not surprising that in 1980 economic reforms figured prominently in the PUWP's approach to yet another political crisis.

However, the events of 1980 differed from the previous crises. First, the strikes were more widespread. Second, the workers were better organized. As Bernhard (1993, p. 201) pointed out, the events of 1980 were preceded by four years of the gradual emergence of organizational networks of oppositional social movements. The workers who participated in these networks became experienced political activists (Bernhard (1993) calls them "a worker counterelite"), capable of shaping spontaneous strikes into a concerted political movement.

The active involvement of intellectuals in the Solidarity movement helped workers to articulate their demands and expand them beyond the immediate concerns, such as wages and consumer prices. Now, the workers demanded the right to participate in political process. The fact that the workers remained organized after the strikes have ended, as well as the spread of the open opposition to other social groups, made the crisis more dangerous for the regime.

The response of the Polish Communists under the leadership of General Jaruzelski was a combination of political oppression and economic reforms. While introducing martial law to eliminate the political opposition and put the PUWP back in control, the regime simultaneously addressed the economic problems by embarking upon the most radical economic reforms in the Soviet bloc.

The discussion on economic reforms started in 1980. Although it was controlled by the PUWP, it included open, professional analysis of the country's economic problems and provided a wide-ranging spectrum of reform proposals.[1] One of the most important results of the reform debate was that the economic views of Solidarity became a part of the officially recognized discourse.

The official reform program, produced in 1981 by the Committee for Economic Reform, was quite radical compared to previous Polish reform attempts, as well as reform programs developed in other Soviet bloc nations. It proposed to replace the existing mechanism of central planning and distribution by direct market relations between producers and consumers. Although the large enterprises remained the property of the state, government control over them was to be limited. Obligatory output plans were to be abolished. Direct-planning targets for enterprises could be issued only to meet the COMECON trade obligations. Central plans remained, but individual enterprises were to be directed toward planned targets by financial instruments and not influenced directly by branch ministries. Indeed, the number of branch ministries was to be sharply reduced: from ten to two. This measure was designed to reduce the branch ministries' ability to micromanage the enterprises. Further diminishing the central administration's influence was the proposed abolition of the intermediate-level industrial amalgamations.

While the reform blueprint envisioned an unprecedented reduction in the central economic administration's ability to influence short-term managerial decisions of individual enterprises, it also made some provisions for decentralization of the long-term investment decisions. Approximately 75% of total investment was to be decentralized to the enterprise level. With very few exceptions, the distribution of material inputs was to be conducted on the bases of direct interenterprise contracts. The inputs that remained centrally rationed were to be distributed by the newly created Supply Bureau (and not by the branch ministries, as used to be the case in the old system).

The reform included drastic changes in the position of enterprises in the economic system. According to the reform blueprint, the main principles of the enterprise's economic activities were to be self-reliance, self-financing, and self-management by workers. These principles were in fact an adaptation of Solidarity's vision of the independent enterprise managed by workers' collective as the primary economic unit. Self-reliance, self-financing, and self-management of enterprises corresponded with the proposed reforms of the central economic apparatus. In general, the economic system presented in the reform blueprint was close to Oscar Lange's model of the market socialist economy. More importantly, its main elements were in agreement with the economic views of Solidarity.

The implementation of the first stage of economic reforms started in the summer of 1981, just several month before the declaration of martial law. Predictably, from the beginning not everything went according to plan. The number of the branch ministries was reduced to five instead of two specified by the reform blueprint. This effectively preserved the traditional administrative structure and severely limited the envisioned autonomy of enterprises. Other compromise solutions, seen as temporary measures, included the direct administrative planning of the production of goods regarded as "critically important" for the economy. The list of such goods was determined by the Bureau of Economic Reform with close involvement of the branch ministries. Prices were divided into three categories: free prices formed by supply and demand were allowed on some goods, while other goods were subject to prices set administratively and those with administratively determined upper limits.

However, despite the inevitable drawbacks, the main elements of reform were implemented. In September 1981 two key laws on enterprise autonomy and self-management were passed by the legislature, thus providing legal foundation for the principles of self-reliance, self-financing, and self-manage-ment of the enterprises that were already being introduced. Tax and legal regulations affecting small state-owned and private firms were liberalized.

Interestingly enough, after the declaration of martial law on December 13, 1981 the regime did not stop the economic reforms. In fact, as Slay (1994) maintains, martial law, by curbing workers' ability to demand wage increases, helped to restore internal economic equilibrium. Thus, the political environ-ment created by martial law had some advantages for the economic reforms were absent during reform attempts of 1956 and 1971. Changes in the foreign trade mechanism, tax and banking systems were implemented in February 1982. These measures increased enterprises' independence vis-a-vis the central economic administration. The first stage of reforms improved Poland's economic performance. In 1983 national income registered the first increase in five years, inflation dropped to 21.4% from 109% in 1982,[2] and hard-currency trade balance showed a 1.44 billion dollars surplus (Slay, 1994, pp. 53, 80). These vital economic indicators continued to show improvement until 1989.

The first stage of economic reforms had created a new financial system for state enterprises, increased the importance of financial instruments, and partly reformed the intermediate level. It also reduced power of the central economic administration, even though the branch ministries managed to retain a significant part of their influence. However, one crucial element of the original reform blueprint was the actual reform policy decisions: the self-management clause had been suspended in December of 1981, shortly after the declaration of martial law. The most important element being removed, the reforms inevitably became yet another attempt to improve performance of the centrally planned economy without changing its nature.

Martial law in Poland ended in July of 1983. The gradual democratiza-tion of the political life that followed was accompanied by the continuing debate on economic reform. The general recognition that the goals of the first stage of economic reform have not been reached and that continuing domination of the branch ministries precluded the economy from reaching higher performance paved the way to the second stage of reforms.

The main goal of the second stage was to improve competitiveness of Polish economy on foreign markets and to create competition between domestic producers. This was to be achieved by establishing the Anti-Monopoly Bureau to prevent excessive industrial concentration and by actively attracting foreign investments for joint ventures. Banking system was to be commercialized by establishing new banks independent of the National Bank of Poland. Enterprises were free to select the bank of their choice. Further liberalization of the foreign trade enabled enterprises to own hard currency proceeds from their income on separate bank accounts.

The implementation of these measures required economic stabilization that in Poland of the 1980s was associated with growing prices combined with stagnant wages. The PUWP lacked the legitimacy needed to persuade the general public in the necessity of these unpopular measures. After the end of martial law the regime could not introduce these measures by force. Attempts to bring the question of the second stage of economic reforms before the voters (and thus legitimize the subsequent price increase) effectively failed when the referendum held in November of 1987 attracted less than 50% of the total number of voters. This made the results invalid and indicated the widespread apathy and distrust in government even when it proposed reasonably sound economic reforms. Attempts to reduce subsidies in 1988 led to increases in prices of food and other basic goods and services. They were followed by a wave of industrial strikes and demands for compensating wage increases. The emerging new crisis threatened political stability. This time, the Polish government could not use economic reforms to diffuse political tensions. The problem could only be addressed by establishing a dialogue with the opposition, that is with the still illegal but nonetheless existing and powerful Solidarity.

The Roundtable Agreements concluded on April 5, 1989 between the government and the opposition (Solidarity had been legalized shortly before the negotiations) opened the door to a rapid democratization of the political process. In June 1989, in the first free post-war parliamentary elections in Poland Solidarity received 260 out of 261 seats. Shortly thereafter the first Polish non-Communist government was formed by Tadeusz Mazowiecki.

The choice of economic experts by the new government signaled a radical departure from the economic reforms designed and implemented in the 1980s. In August 1989 one of the first decisions of Prime Minister Mazowiecki was to appoint Leszek Balcerowicz a deputy prime minister and minister of finance. Balcerowicz, who hitherto had no experience in working with political decision-makers, and who now had become a decision-maker himself, for several years worked on a project of radical economic transformations drawn along the lines of neo-liberal economics. This appointment had an important symbolic significance. By putting Balcerowicz in charge of economic reforms Mazowiecki's government indicated its commitment to a rapid transformation to a capitalist market economy (preferably of the laissez-fair variety).

The blueprint of the Polish economic reforms of the 1980s included provisions for economic stabilization by means of the gradual withdrawal of subsidies and introduction of market prices. They also envisioned the development of the private sector, mostly by attracting foreign investors. The main element of these reforms was decentralization of economic decisions combined with the introduction of enterprise autonomy and workers' self-management. These elements were never fully implemented because the Communist regime lacked legitimacy to introduce unpopular stabilization measures and was unwilling to allow workers' self-management so as not to give too much power to Solidarity. The factors that precluded the full-scale implementation of reforms were of political, rather than economic, nature.

The reform plan proposed by Balcerowicz included the following elements: macroeconomic stabilization, liberalization, and privatization. The emphasis was on the rapid change from socialist to capitalist economic system. The main contrast with the previous economic reform proposals was the rejection of gradualism in favor of what became universally known as "shock therapy". Workers' self-management was not among elements of the Balcerowicz plan. Unlike the reform blueprints of the 1980s, that envisioned a continuous role of the state in the implementation of reforms, this plan maintained that after the initial package of monetary and financial stabilization measures is implemented, the state may step aside and watch the market forces spontaneously transforming the economy. As Slay (1994, p. 89) put it, "implicit in the liberal view was the faith in the market as a socioeconomic institution, both as the *end goal* of the transition (market capitalism) and the *mechanism* for effecting the transition" (*italics in the original*).

Without discussing the merits and drawbacks of the Balcerowicz plan, let us consider the possible motives behind its selection as the policy of economic transformation. The most common account of events leading to the Polish "shock therapy" was originated by the advocates of this policy. Aslund (1992), Sachs and Lipton (1990), Winiecki (1990) were among those who presented the reasons for this choice of economic policy as strictly rational decisions based on strict economic analysis of the existing situation, previous economic reforms, and projected outcomes of the economic transformation. Their argument can be summed up as follows.

The Polish economy in 1989 was on the brink of collapse due to hyperinflation, foreign debt, the disappearance of traditional markets in the Soviet Union. The economic reforms of the 1980s failed because of their poor design. Only a radical break with the past economic policies could help to avoid the economic catastrophe. The only alternative to the Socialist economy was the laissez-fair capitalism and the only way toward it was a rapid, simultaneous, and all-embracing change in all spheres of the economy. Although concise, forceful, and persuasive, this reasoning had one flaw: it assumed what had to be proven. Let us analyze these assumptions point by point.

First, the state of the Polish economy in the 1980s was serious, but certainly not as catastrophic as the above authors would like their audience to believe. For most of the period inflation was contained, its annual rates fluctuating between 14.8% (in 1984) and 61.3% (in 1988). The upsurge of inflation to 243.8% in 1989 was due to the policy of the last Communist government that raised wages to improve its chances in the upcoming elections. Poland's foreign indebtedness increased from 25.2 billion dollars in 1983 to 39.3 billion dollars in 1989 (Slay, 1994). However, the debt was serviced by the proceeds from hard currency exports. Hard currency trade balance was consistently positive throughout the period and in all but one year its surplus exceeded 1 billion dollars. The COMECON still provided a market for low-quality high-cost Polish goods and served as the source of supply of cheap oil and gas. The latter increased the competitiveness of Polish hard-currency exports by reducing production costs. In 1989 nobody could have predicted the COMECON collapse that occurred two years later. One may argue that a threat of the economic collapse was more serious in the crisis of 1979 than it was a decade later. One should also remember that in 1989, unlike 1979, Poland had a government that enjoyed sufficient legitimacy and did not need "economic shock absorbers" to survive.

Economic reforms of the 1980s were a combination of failure and success. They failed when possible changes threatened powerful interest groups whose allegiance was indispensable for the regime. This explains the failure of attempts to reorganize the central economic administration and to eliminate the power of the branch industries. Those elements of reforms that, if implemented, would change the composition of political forces, were removed from the agenda. This applies to the provision of workers' self-management that, although prominently figuring in the official reform blue-print, had never been implemented for fear that it will increase the power of Solidarity. At the same time, the reforms succeeded in making some crucial macroeconomic adjustments. Foreign trade had been liberalized, enabling individual enterprises to enter the foreign (hard-currency) markets directly and to retain a significant share of export revenues. Joint ventures with foreign companies were not only allowed but actively encouraged. The number of centrally distributed consumer and, to a lesser degree, investment goods decreased significantly. In the second stage of reforms the first steps were made toward the commercialization of the banking system and the creation of bond market. The monetary policy became more responsive to the international environment and the requirements of the foreign trade (e.g. the zloty was devalued in 1987 to improve the competitiveness of the Polish exports). Restrictions on cooperation between state-owned enterprises and the private sector were loosened. All these measures lay a foundation for future reforms and greatly facilitated the task of macroeconomic stabilization in the early 1990s.

Thus, neither the state of the Polish economy nor the actual progress of reforms by 1989 suggested that the only alternative to the imminent economic collapse was a "shock therapy" approach to economic transformation. In fact, there was no credible evidence that such an approach would result in any improvement of economic performance. On the other hand, the reforms of the 1980s, with political obstacles to consistent implementation now removed, provided a framework for an effective stabilization program accompanied by structural changes and improved performance. Mazowiecki's government did have a choice between two foundations of the future economic policy. On the one hand there was an untested set of theoretical economic postulates propounded by a team of scholars inexperienced in policy-making. On the other hand, a well elaborated program of reforms, different elements of which were tested with various degrees of success and those elements that remained untested due to political constraints could now be implemented. Given then available knowledge about post-Communist economic transformations, the latter choice would have been more rational, while the former required a leap of faith.

As the above discussion seems to indicate, the choice of the neo-liberal approach to economic reforms could hardly be attributed solely to a rational economic analysis. In order to find the reasons for this choice we should examine cognitive models of the opposition politicians, as well as the changes in legitimation patterns during the last years of Communist rule in Poland.

Prime minister Mazowiecki's political background could hardly contribute to his decision in favor of radical economic reforms. A long-time Catholic intellectual (he was an editor of the Catholic journal *Wiez* and a leading figure in the Club of the Catholic Intelligentsia in the 1970s), he was regarded by the PUWP leadership as more moderate than most of his Solidarity associates. A member of the Polish Sejm in the 1970s, Mazowiecki, together with a group of conservative Catholic deputies (the group was known by its Polish acronym ZNAK), advocated a cooperation between the emerging opposition and the regime. During the strikes of 1980 he favored a negotiated agreement between the workers and the party. Goodwin (1991, p. 27) writes that Mazowiecki "served as a kind of Catholic bridge between sectors of democratic opposition and the party's aspiring reform wing." In 1989, his appointment as a prime minister by General Jaruzielski (then president of Poland) was very much due to his image as a moderate politician who is unlikely to initiate any revolutionary changes.

Most of the opposition intellectuals had more pronounced anti-establishment orientations. They envisioned a society completely free from Communist domination and based on cooperation between self-organized collectivities. As we recall from the discussion in Chapter Two, this vision included the autonomous industrial enterprise managed by workers as the main element of the economic system. However, this attitude started to change after the start of the economic reforms in the early 1980s and especially after the introduction of martial law.

As Kennedy (1991, pp. 163-164) points out, in the years that followed the introduction of martial law, the opposition intellectuals became increasingly interested in free-market theories. It was the interest of political thinkers rather than that of economic experts. Very few of Poland's opposition intellectuals in the 1980s could comprehend the technical side of a sufficiently complex macroeconomic theory (liberal or otherwise). However, they were attracted by the simplicity and seeming logical coherence of the philosophical foundations of neo-liberal economics.

The fact that the economic reforms in Poland coincided with martial law had a major impact on the changes in economic views of the opposition intellectuals (Slay, 1994). They saw that an oppressive political regime can initiate a version of economic reforms not unlike the one they advocated and still not only survive but become even more oppressive. Philosophical works of the leading neo-liberal economists, Hayek and Friedman, that had become available in Poland in the late 1970s, seemed to provide a plausible explanation. In these works, the free market economy is presented as an absolutely necessary condition for a democratic polity and civil society. At the same time any state involvement in the economic processes is seen as a step toward an oppressive and potentially totalitarian regime.

This reasoning was appealing to many Polish intellectuals frustrated by the failure of the anticipated socio-political changes in the wake of the Solidarity strikes of 1980. The neo-liberal economic philosophy gained particular popularity among several key groups within the opposition movement. The Young Poland Movement and its leader Alexander Hall, the group publishing the journal *Res Publica* with Martin Krol as the editor-in-chief, and Antony Macierewicz who was in charge of the newspaper *Glos* are among those listed by Kennedy (1991, p. 382) as proponents of the neo-liberal economic views. *Res Publica* was a journal with conservative perspective, popular among the opposition intelligentsia. *Glos*, originally created by KOR in 1977 to serve as a mouthpiece of various opposition groups, targeted a diverse audience that included both intellectuals and workers. The Young Poland Movement in the 1980s was rapidly expanding its membership among university students and steadily gaining influence within Solidarity. Two prominent publications and the growing student movement facilitated the spread of the new economic philosophy among a wide spectrum of opposition groups.

The neo-liberal economic philosophy became an element of the opposition ideology. Throughout the 1980s the opposition intellectuals concentrated their activities in the political sphere. Therefore, it was convenient to subscribe to a theory that provided the image of a self-regulating and self-perpetuating market that not only takes care of itself but also creates conditions for a democratic development.

Several authors emphasize an essentially ideological nature of the neo-liberal economic agenda of the Polish opposition intellectuals. Pickel (1996, p. 368) points out a surprisingly high degree of consensus among the opposition Polish economists on the issues of market transition. He also notices that this consensus did not follow a significant theoretical discourse. We may add that this is all the more surprising if we recall that the Polish economic thought had a strong tradition of market socialism and that this tradition was widely accepted by the opposition intellectuals. The fact that the paradigm shift from market socialism to laissez-faire capitalism took place without any significant discussion and in the absence of a dialogue between the opposition politicians and the economists supports Pickel's assertion that the neo-liberal economic paradigm acquired the status of an ideological postulate.

Marie Lavigne describes the neo-liberal transition paradigm as a "commitment to the quickest possible move to the market." She continues by stating that this commitment does not suffer critics and that "any objection, even any question, is deemed to come from an opponent of the market, i.e. a die-hard communist" (Lavigne, 1995, p. 249). This kind of argument is characteristic of an ideological construct rather than a theoretical paradigm.

Some studies of post-Communist Poland suggest that liberal capitalism as a part of the newly emerging ideological system is intricately connected to its other elements, namely, anti-Communism and a particular type of Polish nationalism. Wojciech Burszta distinguishes between two Polish nationalist traditions. Both see Communist rule as a system foreign to Polish culture and values and regard it as an aberration of historical process. United in their vision of not so distant past, these two traditions differ in their visions of the future. One concentrates on the uniquely Polish cultural traits and regards their preservation the paramount goal. It views unversalistic institutions, such as the free market, with suspicion, because they may undermine what it perceives as the Polish national community. Another tradition sees Poland as an essentially European society and considers the free market as a means toward the incorporation of the country into the European community (Burszta 1994, pp. 214-215). Needless to say, it is the second tradition that dominated the intellectual discourse in the late 1980s and early 1990s.

Jadwiga Staniszkis suggests that the free market ideology serves to support nationalist aspirations. She writes that in today's Poland nationalism "has its own ideology, formulated in other than nationalistic terms. Paradoxically enough, this is a "Europeanism" with a peculiar vision of Eastern Europe's "return to the real track of history" and with strong Hegelian overtones. The common perception is that such a return is possible only through an imitation of both nineteen-century capitalism and its nation-state organization, both seen as "natural moments of history." (Staniszkis 1992, p. 189).

Andreas Pickel explains the rise of the neo-liberal economic ideology by its Western and decidedly anti-Communist character (Pickel 1996, pp. 369-370). While the latter feature signifies a complete and irrevocable break with the past, the former paints an attractive picture of the future. It is rather ironic that the image of laissez-fair capitalism, attractive as it may be for the Polish reformers, is hardly a reflection of the real economic arrangements in contemporary West European countries.

The plausibility of interpreting neoliberal economic reform programs as ideological constructs strongly influenced by non-economic considerations becomes even more apparent if we consider the actual results of the first two years of the post-Communist market reforms in Poland. Inflation rate actually increased in 1990 and exceeded 350%, while the next year inflation, although having dropped to about 70%, was still higher than in any year between 1983 and 1988. At the same time, gross domestic product declined by 11.6% in 1990 and industrial output declined by 24.2% (instead of the initial projections of decline by 3.1 and 5.0 percent respectively) (Slay, 1994). Judging by the above macroeconomic indicators, the first two years of reforms were hardly an unqualified success. As we shall see in Chapter Four, problems of structural transformation of the Polish economy were even less susceptible to the neo-liberal solutions. Untested economic policies continued, even though at the beginning they seemingly resulted in a sharp decline in economic performance. Such persistence cannot be attributed solely to expectations based on rational economic projections. Even though today we know that these policies proved successful in a longer run, their eventual success was by no means apparent in 1990. Thus, pressing on with economic reforms that produced considerable disruptions for at least two years, instead of the originally promised rapid restructuring and concurrent macroeconomic improvement, the Polish reformers showed that their commitment to market economy went beyond purely economic considerations.

Different Paths to Independence: The Baltics and Belarus

By the end of 1991, Estonia, Latvia, Lithuania, and Belarus each possessed formal attributes of an independent state. This fact, however, should not mask profound differences in the substance of independence between Belarus and the Baltic states, as well as in the internal processes in these republics that led to their secession from the Soviet Union.

In all three Baltic states, the sense of illegitimacy of the Soviet rule had been present, albeit latently, throughout the period when they were constituent Soviet republics. These countries had been incorporated into the Soviet Union by force after their brief existence as independent states between the two world wars. Establishment of the Communist regime brought widespread repression and deportations. At the same time, unlike other Soviet republics, the Baltics did not experience tangible benefits from the Soviet-style industrialization. Prior to their incorporation in the Soviet Union, Estonia, Latvia, and (to a lesser degree) Lithuania had well balanced and relatively prosperous economies with the potential for rapid modernization and growth similar to that experienced by the Scandinavian countries in the post-war years.

Soviet industrialization changed the specialization of the Baltic economies by introducing energy- and material-intensive and environmentally unsafe industries. The increase of demand for labor exceeded the resources available within the Baltic republics and resulted in mass migration of mostly semi-skilled workers from other parts of the Soviet Union. This put pressure on housing construction, utilities and public services that were not always adequately financed by the central authorities. Thus, the Soviet investment policy in the Baltics contributed to a deterioration of living standards for the local population. True, the three Baltic republics enjoyed higher living standards than the rest of the USSR. However, this fact could not serve as an ex post facto justification of their incorporation into the Soviet Union, because the Baltic states had enjoyed an even larger margin of prosperity over their Eastern neighbor when they were independent.

Symbolic underpinnings of Soviet rule in the Baltics were bound to be weaker than in the rest of the USSR. Some symbols, crucial for the value system of the Soviet society, were unlikely to invoke positive feelings among many Balts. The October Revolution and the civil war that followed it in the Baltics did not result in victory for the revolutionaries and thus was not easy to glorify. Industrialization did not produce the same increase in upward social mobility as in other republics. The Great Patriotic War, a symbol of enormous significance in the Soviet ideology, was perceived by many Balts not as a victory over forces of evil, but rather as a confusing sequence of three occupations (Soviet - German - Soviet), each bringing repression and hardship.[3]

The ruling Communist elite in the Baltics realized that the standard Soviet system of sacred symbols was not working in their republics and, therefore, more effective symbols should be used to legitimize their rule. They found that appeal to national sentiments, shared language, history, and culture can serve as a basis for legitimation. In the 1950s and 1960s, Communist leaders in Estonia, Latvia, and Lithuania combined loyalty to the Communist ideology with deliberate and successful defence of their national cultures. Sniechkus in Lithuania, Berklavs in Latvia, Kaebin in Estonia -- all these Communist leaders managed to establish a sense of legitimacy of their rule among their people by appealing to the shared national, rather than official Soviet, symbols.[4] This policy secured their personal position vis-a-vis their constituencies. To some degree, it might have strengthened the authority of local Communist parties. However, it is unlikely that it contributed to legitimation of the Soviet regime in the Baltics.

Numerous examples of the Communist leadership participation in the Baltic independence movements in the late 1980s indicate that nationalist ideas survived even among those people who were supposed to be obedient executors of the policy of Soviet internationalism. In Latvia, the veteran National-Communist Berklavs became the head of the Latvian National

Party, while the last Latvian Communist Party Secretary Anatolijs Gorbunovs was working closely with the Latvian Popular Front and successfully moved into the post-Soviet politics with the latter's support. In Estonia, the Estonian Communist Party daily *Rahva Haal* was the first to publish the secret protocols of the Molotov-Ribbentrop Pact, whose existence the Soviet authorities kept silent for more than forty years.[5] In Lithuania, Algirdas Brazauskas, the Lithuanian Communist Party leader and career Soviet apparatchik, started a movement for secession of the local Communist Party from the CPSU. These and many other examples of active support for the national independence by the Soviet ruling elite in the Baltics are well documented and described (for a detailed description, see e.g., Lieven, 1993, Nahaylo and Swoboda, 1990) and therefore there is no need to dwell upon them here. Suffice it to say that policies of the ruling elites in the Baltics throughout the Soviet rule, as well as their behavior when this rule was crumbling, suggest that the idea of national independence was supported by a significant part of the Soviet and Party cadres in the Baltics.

The attitudes of the Communist officials provided a relatively secure environment for the nationally minded intelligentsia. In the previous chapter we described how the nationalist leaders were able to recruit experts from the academic establishment with relative ease. The nationalist leaders themselves were not outcasts, but rather successful members of artistic and academic elites, as well (especially in Lithuania and Estonia) high-level administrative establishment. Even for the moderate intellectuals, who did not favor the immediate cessation from the USSR, national independence was of paramount value and the illegitimacy of the Soviet rule in the Baltics was obvious. Their attitude can be summed up in a statement by Mikhail Bronshtein, a prominent Estonian economist: "The first truth is that the independence of the Baltic countries, and Estonia first of all, had to be recognized. Because what happened there in 1940 was a crime -- an act of banditry identical to Saddam Hussein's in Kuwait. Without independence there could be no normal course of future development in the Baltic region. The second truth is that, to the degree that the issue of independence and sovereignty is resolved, that of preserving economic integration will become increasingly acute, because the greatest danger for the former Soviet republics is that of disintegration." (Bronshtein, 1993, p. 513). The statement clearly sets the priorities typical for the moderate Baltic intellectuals: continuing economic cooperation with the former Soviet republics is desirable, but national sovereignty has a paramount importance.

Among the general public, the overt expression of desire for national independence grew as the disintegration of the Soviet power structures accelerated. Positive attitude toward the brief period of national independence in the 1920s and 1930s was an important foundation for legitimation of the future national sovereignty. Interestingly enough, positive perception of the Baltic independent states prior to the Soviet takeover was widespread not only among the older generation, who might have had personal memories of that period, but among the younger generation as well. A survey of the university students in 1989 showed that attitude toward the first emergence of the independent Baltic states as the most important positive event in national history was expressed by 93% of Estonians, 53% of Lithuanians and 34% of Latvians (Novikova et al., 1989). Conversely, perception of the Molotov-Ribbentrop pact of 1939 as the most important negative event was equally distributed. The Soviet regime in the Baltics was routinely referred to as a foreign military occupation in the nationalist press and speeches of the nationalist leaders during mass rallies and demonstrations. The persistence of such characterization suggests that it was shared by the general public.

As the nationalist forces in the Baltics realized that their actions will not result in an immediate and crushing oppression by the central authorities, they did not hesitate to vent their feelings of illegitimacy of the Soviet rule in public. From April 1987 through May 1988 more than 21 demonstrations occurred throughout the Baltics that raised secessionist demands, most of them attracting from a few hundred participants to ten thousand (Beissinger, 1996, p. 114). In the years that followed, the impressive displays of nationalist sentiments became more numerous and attracted larger numbers of participants. One of the most impressive events of this sort was the so called "Baltic Way", when on August 23, 1989, on the fiftieth anniversary of the Molotov-Ribbentrop pact, some two million people in Lithuania, Latvia, and Estonia formed a human chain stretching from Vilnius to Tallinn to show their solidarity in the opposition to the Soviet rule in the Baltics. Later that year, the general sense of illegitimacy of the forcible incorporation into the USSR was expressed in legal terms when the Estonian Supreme Council (formed before the democratic electoral reform) declared Soviet annexation of Estonia in 1940 illegal.

The Lithuanian Supreme Council declared independence on March 11, 1990. This move was followed by similar declarations by the Latvian and Estonian Supreme Councils a week later. In all three Baltic states, especially in Lithuania and Latvia, these actions marked the beginning of a prolonged and sometimes violent confrontation with Moscow that lasted for more than a year and culminated in a military assault by Soviet forces on government buildings in Vilnius in the winter of 1991. This particular event was probably the harshest test of the Lithuanian people's will for independence as well as of the coherence of the nationalist leadership. For more than a month thousands of armed Soviet soldiers, supported by tanks and armored personnel carriers, were camped in the center of Vilnius, where they seized the central television station. They several times tried to capture the buildings of the Lithuanian government and legislature, but were repeatedly stopped by crowds of unarmed Lithuanians who would not give way even though on one occasion thirteen of them were crushed to death by tanks. Fearing that a larger number of victims might tarnish the democratic-reformist image of the Gorbachev government, Moscow authorities called off the assault.

However, the military standoff continued for some time. Numerous acts of intimidation were undertaken by the Soviet military and police forces against Latvia and Estonia throughout spring and summer of 1991. All this was to no avail: referenda in all three states resulted in overwhelming majorities voting for independence.

In Estonia, Latvia, and Lithuania national independence was the result of deliberate actions, initiated by the nationally minded part of the ruling elite and intellectuals and supported by a majority of the general public. The idea of national independence was well established in all social strata and partly based on a widely shared conviction of the illegitimacy of the Soviet rule in the Baltics. It had decidedly anti-Soviet (although not necessarily anti-Communist) and anti-Russian overtones. In Belarus, national independence vis-a-vis the rest of the USSR and Russia in particular had quite a different place in the system of shared national symbols. This system was heavily influenced by relations with Russia and the USSR, as well as Poland, in the twentieth century.

After the revolution of 1917 and the civil war, in the Eastern part of Byelorussia, Soviet authorities created the Byelorussian Soviet Socialist Republic (BSSR) as one of the constituent republics of the Soviet Union. In the twenties Soviet Communist leaders conducted a policy beneficial to the non-Russian minorities of the USSR. In Byelorussia, this policy resulted in the purposeful and consistent campaign of Byelorussization. Significant resources were allocated for the introduction of the Byelorussian language into education on all levels, from elementary schools to universities, into the mass media as well as the administrative system.

The development of Byelorussian literature and Byelorussian culture in general was officially supported and accompanied by radical changes in the ethnic composition of the social hierarchy. Native Byelorussians were recruited to various positions in the administrative system and given an opportunity to acquire university degrees and subsequently to form the new educated elite. These actions filled the previously existing gap between the rural population (predominantly Byelorussian) and elite groups (either Polish or Russian). Now, Byelorussians occupied all levels of the social hierarchy, from the bottom to the top.

Another consequence of this policy was an increase in national consciousness of Byelorussians. Literacy increased, newspapers published in Byelorussian became available even in remote villages, and peasants now often had personal contacts with cities and towns through those members of their communities who moved to urban centers for an education or a job. Byelorussians in the cities, towns, and villages now perceived themselves not as just "locals" but as members of the Byelorussian nation. Later the official Soviet ideologues often invoked memories of this period in order to support a claim that Byelorussia owes its national existence to the Soviet rule. Although such statements are exaggerated, it is true that under Soviet rule in the 1920s Byelorussia enjoyed substantially more national independence than when it was a mere administrative unit in the Russian Empire. It is also true that upward mobility of Byelorussians under Soviet rule markedly exceeded that in Western Byelorussian territories under Polish control.

The Soviet policy of fostering Byelorussia's national development proved to be short-lived. Its abandonment in the thirties was followed in Byelorussia by brutal reprisals against the national intelligentsia, ban on the books and journals which were considered too nationalist, and persecution of the new Byelorussian elites. Even devoted Communists were purged if they were suspected of being nationally-minded.[6] However, these repressions failed to reverse the course of Byelorussian national development. Byelorusssian national consciousness had already been awakened, and participation of ethnic Byelorussians in administration and intellectual life continued.

Although Byelorussia was subjected to collectivization in the thirties, the policy was conducted less brutally than in many other parts of the USSR. Unlike Ukraine, no famine was deliberately organized by the Soviet authorities. Industrialization was not conducted on a large scale in Byelorussia before the war. This was probably due to the fact that Byelorussia was located on the border with Poland, a location that made industry vulnerable to enemy attack in case of war.

An outcome of the delayed industrialization was that the Byelorussian rural community remained very much intact and rural-urban migration was not as extensive as in the rest of the USSR. Rural communities, with their traditional cultural patterns, retained their role in Byelorussian culture. Another consequence was that latent opposition to the Communist rule in Byelorussia was not so widespread as in the neighboring Ukraine.

Western Byelorussia was under Polish control until September of 1939. In general, the Polish authorities were hostile to the Byelorussian national idea, persistently conducting a policy of Polonization.[7] Byelorussian language and culture survived in rural communities, and in the cities a few nationalist intellectuals were trying against all odds to maintain the Byelorussian national identity above the communal level.[8] It is interesting to note that the Polish authorities were much more willing to accept the preservation of the Byelorussian culture on the local level than development of the Byelorussian national consciousness on the societal level.[9]

Just as in Soviet Byelorussia, in Western Byelorussia problems of modernization were not acute; it was the least industrialized region of Poland. Thus, by the end of the thirties, to the west of the border as well as to the east of it, the rural community remained a primary sanctuary of the inchoate Byelorussian nationality.

The hostile attitude of the Polish authorities to the Byelorussian national development accounts for the fact that the native Byelorussian population of Western Byelorussia welcomed the Soviet invasion in September 1939.[10] Unlike the citizens of the independent Baltic states, Western Byelorussians did not perceive this forcible unification with the Soviet Union as an infringement upon their national rights. At first, deceived by Soviet propaganda, they looked at the invaders as liberators; later, when the real nature of the Soviet regime became clear, they simply considered them as just another oppressor that simply happened to be more brutal than the previous ones.

German invasion also was at first met as a liberation from Soviet rule (both in Western and Eastern Byelorussia).[11] However, the short-sighted and dogmatic racial policy of the Nazis, atrocities committed during the extermination of the Jews, and violent reprisals against the local population suspected of sabotage or guerilla activities, resulted in disappointment and later in widespread resistance. Byelorussian terrain, with its swamps and dense forests, was well suited for partisan warfare, and partisan units in Byelorussia were more numerous and more active than in other Soviet territories occupied by the Germans.

Partisan warfare had important consequences for the development of Byelorussian social structure and contributed to certain peculiarities of officially recognized value-patterns. First, armed resistance created a favorable image of Byelorussia within the Soviet ideological framework. Byelorussia was often referred to as the "partisan republic". Now, Byelorussia was able to identify itself within the existing symbolic system and to find the only possible source of national self-esteem at a time when all other sources were either forgotten or forbidden. Second and even more important, a new generation of Byelorussian leaders emerged from commanders of the partisan units.

By the end of the German occupation of Byelorussia, most of the partisan fighters and commanders were of local origin. The specific character of guerilla warfare implied that for success and survival such qualities were instrumental as initiative, ability to gain the confidence and support of the local population, pragmatic rather than an ideological approach to the problems.

After the war, successful partisan commanders were often recruited to various positions in the party and administrative apparatus. There they naturally retained those qualities which helped them to succeed during the war. They also retained close, sometimes personal, ties with their native communities and often used their positions to help them. Gradually moving to the highest levels of the bureaucratic hierarchy, former guerilla leaders became the dominant group in the Byelorussian leadership by the early sixties and remained in this position for about twenty years, thus having an important impact on the development of modern Byelorussia.

The commitment of this generation of the Byelorussian leaders to the welfare of their republic, their sense of responsibility to the local population (the latter being more likely a vestige of communal value-orientation than a result of political maturity), together with the ability to attain their goals through unorthodox means to some extent account for the relative prosperity of the post-war Byelorussia. In the Soviet administrative system it was very important to be able to bargain for centrally distributed resources. The qualities the Byelorussian leaders acquired during their participation in partisan warfare proved useful in persuading the central Soviet authorities that more resources should be given to Byelorussia and fewer taken away from the republic. In this bargaining they did not hesitate to invoke images of Byelorussia devastated by the war, of the heroic struggle of the Byelorussian people against the Germans and of their own experiences in this struggle. They continued to benefit from these ideologically sacred symbols for thirty years after the war ended.

However, their vision of what was good for the republic was shaped by the general attitude of the Soviet ruling elite. Large-scale industrialization, regardless of all social and environmental consequences, became the first priority for Byelorussia after the war. In a short time many large industrial enterprises were built, most of them completely dependent on supplies from other regions of the USSR. Rapid modernization dramatically increased migration from rural areas to the cities which resulted in labor shortages in agricultural production. Chemical plants and oil refineries, which were among the most attractive symbols of modernity for the Byelorussian leadership, were environmentally unsafe and used raw materials shipped from remote parts of the Soviet Union.

True, living standards in Byelorussia, in terms of food and other consumer goods supply, were somewhat higher than in many other republics. On the other hand, this relative well-being could be achieved only at a certain cost. Byelorussian leaders tried to gain what they considered of primary importance and did not care that they were forced to sacrifice things they hardly considered important at all, namely, Byelorussian language, Byelorussian culture, Byelorussian national identity in general.

Byelorussia became the testing ground for Russification under the guise of "internationalization". The number of Byelorussian schools was dwindling; in other schools Byelorussian language and literature were becoming a less and less significant part of the curriculum. By the early 1970s, in Minsk, the capital of Byelorussia and a city with population about one million, no school used Byelorussian as the language of instruction (Kennedy, 1991, p. 167). Not a single high school textbook on the pre-revolutionary history of Byelorussia had been published in the post-war years. In the officially allowed studies of Byelorussian history some crucial topics were deliberately ignored. For example, a student of the Uniate Church in Belarus (the majority of Byelorussians belonged to this church before its abolition by the Russian authorities in 1839) would have to rely exclusively on the Polish sources, since no detailed study of this subject has been published in Belarus.

It is hard to imagine that in any other Soviet republic such a blatant attack against a nation's language, culture, and history could have passed unopposed. However, in Byelorussia there was no manifest public opposition to this process. I would suggest that there are three basic reasons for this. First, the Russian language was associated with upward social mobility and modernity. Second, Byelorussian culture had been oppressed for centuries (except for a short period in the 1920s); now, at least, cultural oppression coincided with improving material conditions. Third, despite being dismantled on the societal level, Byelorussian national identity still retained its traditional sanctuary on the communal level in rural areas.[12] All this, together with a feeling of being materially better off than many other republics, made the situation acceptable for most of the Byelorussian population. This pragmatic policy of the Byelorussian leaders was quite successful, at least in the short run.

However, the "partisan" generation of the Byelorussian leaders began to leave the scene in the early eighties, being gradually replaced by the *apparatchiks* and technocrats of the late Brezhnev era.[13] The "partisan" generation of administrators usually had no managerial industrial experience and maintained close personal relations with their native communities. By contrast, the industrialists did not have intimate ties with the rural communities and were interested in the expansion of production for its own sake, regardless of the social and environmental consequences. Their enterprises had numerous connections with other enterprises around the Soviet Union. Their upward mobility did not require retention of their national identity. On the contrary, it was quite convenient to belong to a vague group of the "Russian-speaking people". Both technological ties with other regions and career aspirations made the idea of Byelorussian national independence of any kind absolutely alien. Michael Urban in his study of the Byelorussian elites states that an almost complete absence of nationalist sentiment among them makes Belarus an ideal case for the study of the typical Soviet elite formation. In particular he notes that the latest generation of the ruling elite did not possess a well-defined and articulated sense of national identity (Urban, 1989, p.16).

The attitude of the Byelorussian ruling elite toward the general public is exemplified in statements by the Byelorussian prime-minister, Viacheslav Kebich, who in his nostalgic reminiscences of Pyotr Masherov, a leader of Byelorussian Communist Party during the Brezhnev's period, constructed his ideal of a "real Byelorussian" as someone who works hard, demands nothing and does not criticize his superiors (Kebich, 1993).

Industrial leaders were routinely elected to legislative bodies of various levels (such as oblast Soviets and the Byelorussian Supreme Soviet). Actually, they did not need those seats as long as their legislative power was negligible. However, their strong electoral positions proved useful during the last years of the Soviet Union and after its collapse.

Elections to the Byelorussian Supreme Soviet in the spring of 1990 revealed the weakness of the nationalist opposition. Out of 345 candidates elected to the Supreme Soviet only 27 were members of the Byelorussian Popular Front. On the other hand, more than two hundred seats were occupied by directors of large enterprises, high ministerial executives, and regional administrators.

Thus, the processes that had led to independence in the Baltics and Belarus were quite different. In the Baltics, national independence was regarded as a legitimate goal by significant groups within every social stratum, including the ruling elite. Independence in Estonia, Latvia, and Lithuania was achieved as a result of deliberate, concerted and sustained actions, constantly testing the limits of Soviet tolerance. For the majority of the Baltic population national independence came to occupy a central place in the system of shared values. For the decision-makers, national sovereignty served as a value-induced cognitive constraint, thus reducing the number of feasible choices in making decisions regarding economic policies.

Byelorussians did not develop a salient anti-Russian sentiment, partly because in the post-revolutionary period Russians did not threaten Byelorussian culture at the communal level. In the twenties, they even permitted it to expand to the societal level. Until the recent upsurge of environmental problems and environmental awareness, Byelorussians were quite happy with the results of industrialization and economic relations with Russia. Modern society in Byelorussia was perceived as predominantly Russian, intrinsically connected with Russian language and Russian culture. Byelorussians were free to enter this society as long as they were willing to adopt at least some features of the Russian national identity.

The legitimation pattern in Byelorussia for centuries was characterized by ambivalent compliance. It was a curious modification of traditional type of legitimation, tradition to comply with any force. This tradition somewhat changed during the rule of "partisan" leaders who were seen not as representatives of an outside power but rather as "locals" who cared about their people. But in general ambivalent compliance prevailed.

In Belarus (the new name adopted in 1991), independence had been received rather than achieved. Its emergence as a sovereign state was not accompanied by successful actions by mass nationalist movements or circulation of the ruling elites. Byelorussian decision-makers, unlike their counterparts in the Baltics, tended to regard national sovereignty not as an end but as a means, not as a constraint on their set of choices but rather as a variable within this set. These differences in attitudes toward national independence between the Baltic states and Belarus proved to be crucial for the shape of the early stages of post-Soviet economic reforms, when politicians and experts in these four countries were faced with very similar economic problems.

Economic Consequences of Independence

There are three groups of factors that had been set in motion by the processes associated with the emergence of the former Soviet republics as newly independent countries. Each of these groups influenced the new national economies in its own particular way. At the same time, each group had a similar impact on all four former Soviet republics in our sample.

The first group of factors represents the economic pressure by the Soviet authorities (Russian authorities after the Soviet collapse) on their neighbors to achieve political or economic concessions. The second group was of a purely economic nature and was caused by the disappearance of the old Soviet system of central administrative bodies that regulated both interenterprise and interregional (interrepublican) exchange. The resulting spontaneous realignment of economic units had painful effect both on the fledgling national economies and on many enterprises, especially in the secondary sector. The third group of factors was a direct result of independence, whereupon the newly independent states had to assume responsibility for budget, credit and monetary policies formerly conducted by the central authorities.

The Baltic states first experienced the impact of Soviet economic pressure after they declared their independence in the spring of 1990. A month after the declaration, Moscow responded by cutting off the oil supply, as well as by delaying shipments of raw materials vital for the Baltic economies. In addition to that, the Central Bank of the USSR stopped the supply of money to the three Baltic countries, thus creating chaos in their monetary systems. The Soviet economic blockade lasted for four months. When the Lithuanian Supreme Council accepted a moratorium on the declaration of independence and similar concessions had been made by the other Baltic states, supplies from the rest of the USSR resumed.

However, the fact that Moscow succeeded in forcing the Balts into concessions by means of economic pressure encouraged the Russian authorities to undertake similar actions in the future. In January of 1992, a drastic reduction of oil supplies to Estonia resulted in the resignation of the Prime Minister Edgar Savisaar. Ironically, he was much less hostile toward Moscow than his successor, Mart Laar. Thus, the manipulation with oil supplies, although a source of formidable Russian influence, proved to be too indiscriminate to achieve specific political objectives. In general, sporadic interruptions of oil and other energy sources supplies to the Baltics seemed to be acts of sheer vindictiveness rather than a rational power politics. After the collapse of the Soviet Union, Russia failed to force significant concessions out of the Balts by manipulating oil supplies.

In the case of Belarus, oil supplies at relatively low prices (above the internal Russian prices but still below those of the world market) were actively and successfully used to influence internal political processes. Usually, even a promise of additional oil shipments would boost the popularity of the Byelorussian leaders by proving their ability to obtain the resources necessary for the continuing operation of the economy. In turn Russia was assured that Belarus remained in its sphere of influence and, when necessary, would take actions that benefitted Russia. For example, Belarus established custom and passport controls on its borders with Latvia, Lithuania, and Ukraine which created an impediment for the development of trade with these countries and served Russia's goal to isolate them. Belarus did not charge Russia for the use of military bases on its territory. Russia was allowed a free transit of goods through Belarus, an important economic concession since most Russian oil and gas exports are shipped to Europe through the Byelorussian pipelines.

Russia was able to use oil as a means of intimidation (in the case of the Baltics) and inducement (in the case of Belarus) for the purposes of foreign policy (however ill-defined) because the oil industry was at least partly controlled by the Russian state, both directly, through a share of government ownership in large oil and gas consortiums, and indirectly, through export licenses. At the same time, the central authorities in the late Soviet Union and its successor states, including Russia, were rapidly losing control over the bulk of the industry, especially the intricate network of interenterprise supplies. For small republics with a high share of manufacturing industries in their national economies, this spontaneous process had consequences even more serious than those of Russia's deliberate manipulations of oil supplies and prices.

Within the Soviet Union, the division of labor between the constituent republics was imposed from the center and controlled by the central authorities. The main task of coordination was assigned to the All-Union industrial ministries. They directed exchange between enterprises. The regional aspect of coordination of exchange was carried out by the State Planning Committee of the USSR that controlled balances of trade between the republics. Exchanges between enterprises were of primary importance and subject to constant control and coordination, while interrepublican trade was mostly reflected in ex post facto statistical analyses. Central authorities would intervene in the interrepublican trade only to ensure the adequate supply of basic foodstuffs, consumer goods, and energy. The system was inefficient, but when it disappeared with the collapse of the Soviet Union, there was no immediate replacement of even comparable efficiency.

With the disappearance of the central authorities, links between enterprises remained. Over the years, the management of every industrial enterprise established close relations with suppliers and buyers. The Soviet economy being a closed system with a deliberately limited number of monopolist producers (and a correspondingly limited number of monopsonist consumers), individual enterprises had a limited choice of potential buyers or suppliers. Even with a significantly diminishing capacity of central authorities to control interenterprise exchange, enterprises had to remain within the existing network. This situation changed precipitously when enterprises were allowed to conduct international transactions independently of the Ministry of Foreign Trade, as long as they obtained export license. Now, enterprises of the primary sector had strong incentives to enter the world market of raw materials that promised much higher prices than those that traditional buyers in the former USSR and COMECON could offer.   By contrast, manufacturing enterprises found themselves in a predicament: to ensure a regular supply of energy and raw materials they had to pay world prices (preferably in hard currency); to obtain hard currency, they had to export their products; to compete successfully on international markets with products of low quality, they had to reduce prices; the high price of energy and raw materials increased their production costs above the price at which their products would sell.

Even though the primary sector producers could obtain export licenses for limited amounts of their products and had to sell the rest on the domestic market, the new situation reduced the reliable supply and increased prices. This started a chain reaction of supply disruption exacerbated by the highly monopolistic nature of the Soviet economy. One factor alleviated the severity of the problem: enterprises typically had significant stockpiles of raw materials and constituent parts which they could use for some time. But this relief was only temporary.

Both Belarus and the Baltic states have a very limited number of primary sector enterprises. Most of their industries are high on the technological chain, usually producing finished goods. Thus they suffered equally from the spontaneous disruption of supplies. In 1992, Mario Nuti and Jean Pisani-Ferry estimated that the disruption of interrepublican trade would cost Belarus, Estonia, and Latvia each about 52 percent of its net material product, while

Lithuania was to lose about 46 percent (quoted in Williamson, 1993). Russia, with its massive primary sector, would lose only about 11 percent of its net material product (Ibid.). However imprecise,[14] these calculations reflect the fact that of all the republics Russia was in the strongest bargaining position vis-a-vis its neighbors.[15]

The disintegration of the former Soviet system of distribution and subsequent financial losses among enterprises of the secondary sector forced many of them into what technically could be described as insolvency. The only reason they did not go bankrupt was a peculiar process of accumulating interenterprise debts that came to be known as the crisis of arrears. In the Soviet economy all transactions between enterprises were cleared only through the central bank and its territorial branches. This changed with the emergence of commercial banks and the introduction of new laws on banking that allowed enterprises to clear their accounts directly or to engage in trade credit operations. Those enterprises whose finances were destroyed by decreasing revenues and rising costs could not expect the state to completely restore their solvency, because the state had to tighten budget constraints. Instead, to maintain a semblance of operational normalcy, they resorted to the inflated trade credit.

Instead of clearing accounts with timely payments, enterprise would issue IOUs to their debtors, who in turn would do the same in regard to their debtors, and so forth. As Ickes and Ryterman (1992) indicate, these operations differed significantly from the normal practice of trade credit. Usually, an enterprise would resort to trade credit to replenish its working capital when it does not have access to a bank. Therefore, interest rates are higher than the normal ones, reflecting the higher potential risk. In the case of the former Soviet enterprises, interest rates on interenterprise debts were typically close to zero, which, taking into account high inflation, translated into negative interest rates. This behavior is of a decidedly non-market nature and so are explanations of it. First, the management of industrial enterprises understood that the state would not enforce the laws on bankruptcy (by 1992 such laws, in one form or another, had been adopted in all former Soviet republics). Second, while defaulting on their debts to each other, the enterprises demonstrated their inability to pay state taxes and thus forced the state to provide modified soft budget constraints by not collecting tax revenues. Third, as we shall see in the discussion that follows, some factors of the crisis of arrears had been set in motion directly by the collapse of the Soviet Union.

For some time after they became independent, all former Soviet republics had to use the Russian ruble as the sole legal tender for all transactions (belonged to the "ruble zone"). At the same time, banking was decentralized, with national banks in individual countries replacing the republican divisions of the former Soviet Central Bank and commercial banks appearing in large numbers. This devolution of the banking system meant that all non-cash payments between enterprises located in different countries had to be cleared through bilateral corresponding accounts in their central banks. The introduction of this procedure resulted in increased delays in payments. Routine transactions that used to take several days prior to the dissolution of the banking system now took as long as two months (Ickes and Ryterman, 1993, p. 349).

Despite the emergence of independent national banks in former Soviet republics, since all of them were in the ruble zone, only the Russian National bank could conduct the emission of notes, while non-cash money emission was controlled by each independent national bank. This situation meant that former republics had to rely on Russia for their money supply. The centralized supply of Russian rubles from the Russian National Bank was never in the quantities needed by the newly independent economies for normal volumes of cash transactions. Cash-strapped enterprises had to use their cash reserves to pay wages to their employees. Thus, cash payment as the speediest way of interenterprise transactions was not an option available to most enterprises.

The combination of the decentralized banking system and centralized money supply contributed to the crisis of arrears. Ironically, the tightening of money supply by the Russian Central bank, a measure designed to combat inflation, added inflationary pressure on economies in all countries of the ruble zone. Even profitable enterprises that would otherwise have been in a sound financial situation were forced to default on their debts by delays in non-cash transactions and the lack of cash for a timely clearing of accounts. They had to rely on the state to remain afloat. Sooner or later the state would help them by providing the necessary credit which in turn would very soon translate into an additional influx of cash into the economy.

This would not have had a damaging effect had the state rescued only financially viable enterprises that encountered serious but temporary problems due to circumstances beyond their control. However, the universality of the crisis of arrears obscured the real performance of each enterprise. Both profitable enterprises and loss-makers found themselves technically insolvent. This frustrated the first attempts at industrial restructuring by depriving the authorities of the information necessary to evaluate and compare the performance of different enterprises. An even more important consequence was that state support of insolvent enterprises put additional strain on budget and monetary systems that already had to meet the needs created by the newly acquired independence.

Under the Soviet system, budgets of the constituent republics played a limited role. The bulk of revenues originating in the republics was transferred to the central All-Union budget. Funds necessary for local expenditures were transferred back to the republics. It is estimated that prior to the collapse of the USSR, Belarus and the Baltic states transferred about 40 percent of their respective GDPs to the central budget (IMF, 1993).

The budget had the following principal sources of revenue: enterprise profits,[16] turnover tax,[17] individual income tax, social security payments. Profits of all-Union enterprises, as well as social security contributions by both all-Union and republican enterprises, were transferred directly to Moscow. Significant portions of turnover and personal income taxes were transferred to Moscow via republican budgets. The only independent quasi-fiscal base of the republics was represented by the profits of republican enterprises. The budgetary system that channelled revenues to the central budget and then allotted funds to cover republics' expenditures was an important element of the highly centralized Soviet economic system.

After independence, both revenue and expenditure profiles in the Baltics and in Belarus changed sharply. First, they did not have to transfer their revenues to Moscow. Second, they were not supposed to expect payments from Moscow. Independence meant, among other things, independent budgets. At first sight it might seem that Belarus and the Baltic states should benefit from the new arrangement, since they had a large share of industries that produced higher than average added value and had correspondingly high profit margins. According to many estimates (e.g., IMF, 1993c), under the Soviet system republics with this composition of industry transferred more funds to the central budget than they received from it. Now they had the revenue base that in theory was sufficient to cover their budget expenditures, provided the expenditure profile remained the same. The real situation with both revenues and expenditures proved to be quite different.

First, the large all-Union enterprises were the most seriously affected by the crisis of arrears described above. Defaulting on their debts, they declared their inability to pay their dues to the newly independent states. The latter did not have an adequate system of tax collection to replace the old system of profit transfers to the central budget. Nor did they possess a working system of the turnover tax collection. The problem with turnover tax (now renamed and partly restructured into VAT and excise taxes) was exacerbated by the changing nature of commercial activities and, correspondingly, spending patterns. More people than before were buying goods and services in the expanding "black market" which was tolerated but not yet officially recognized. Obviously the state was unable to collect taxes from the unregistered black market merchants. Adding to the general chaos in the revenue part of the budget, the social security contributions of the Baltic states (but not of Belarus) were frozen by Russia immediately after the dissolution of the Soviet Union.

While the revenues proved to be much smaller than expected, expenditures actually increased. First, republics now had to finance education, health care and other social services that had been centrally funded under the Soviet system. Defence expenses represented one of the completely new expenditures for the newly independent states. Money for pensions, frozen in the Russian central bank, had to be provided by the respective governments of the Baltic states. And, probably worst of all, large industrial enterprises, instead of being sources of revenue, were now insolvent and demanded government assistance.

Another unexpected addition to the budget expenditures was caused by the dramatically rising prices of oil and gas imported from Russia. We have already mentioned the impact of rising oil prices on industrial enterprises. However, Belarus and the Baltics depended entirely on Russian oil and gas supplies, not only for continuing industrial activity but also for the production of heat and electricity for households. In December 1991, the price of Russian oil was 70 rubles per ton both for the domestic Russian market and for export to Belarus and the Baltic region. Six month later, Russia's domestic oil price increased to 2,000 rubles per ton. Its oil export price to the Baltics rose to 6,243 rubles per ton (Shen, 1994, p. 176). To ensure at least a minimal supply of electricity and heat to households, the Baltic governments had to pay for shipments of the Russian oil directly from their budgets.

The growing gap between decreasing budget revenues and increasing budget expenditures contributed to the rising inflation. For the first two years after the dissolution of the USSR, Russia was the only country in the ruble zone that could conduct monetary emission.[18] This restricted the inflationary potential of other newly independent states and channelled their inflationary activities mostly to the extension of the negative interest rate credit to industrial and agricultural enterprises. However, even this limitation was steadily loosening as inflation in Russia was rapidly growing, thus allowing more cash to be imported into the newly independent states.

Rapid credit expansion was accompanied by the price liberalization that in Belarus and the Baltics started in 1991. It was intended to translate the repressed inflation, typical for the Soviet-type economies, into the overt infla-tion. The benefits of such a move were supposed to be twofold. First, the shortages (the main feature of the repressed inflation) would be eliminated. Second, unlike the repressed inflation, the overt inflation can be measured with relative ease and precision. However, the decrease in the repressed inflation proved to be short-lived. Since the producers retained their monopolist positions, they did not feel the pressure to reduce costs and increase outputs. Instead, they kept output constant and were increasing costs, as well as profit margins (sometimes indistinguishable from costs in the Soviet accounting practice). The former contributed to the continuing shortages (repressed inflation) while the latter added the cost-push element into the overt inflationary process. As Shteinbuka (1993, p. 494) points out in her analysis of the reforming Baltic economies, there was no inverse relationship between prices and the deficit. In 1991, with prices rising, the deficit was somewhat reduced for a limited number of items, while most goods remained in short supply. The official Byelorussi an statistical agency reported that in 1991 the increase in profits of industrial enterprises had been achieved solely by rising prices, while keeping output constant or even reducing it (State Statistical Committee of the Republic of Belarus, 1992).

The budgetary credit expansion and the cost-push inflation caused by monopolist enterprises combined led to hyperinflation in all four countries in the first year of post-Soviet transformation. In 1991 annual rates of inflation exceeded 200 percent in Lithuania, Latvia, Estonia, and Belarus. In 1992, inflation in all three Baltic states exceeded one thousand percent, while in Belarus it was 765 percent (Shen, 1994).

John Maynard Keynes, observing the hyperinflation in Central Europe immediately after World War One, said that "there is no subtler, no surer means of overturning the existing basis of Society than to debauch the currency. The process engages all the hidden forces of economic law on the side of destruction, and does it in a manner which not one man in a million is able to diagnose" (Keynes, 1919 (1963), p. 78). Seventy years later, post-Soviet governments, because of necessity, weakness, or incompetence, engaged in the same destructive practices.

One of the most damaging features of the monetary policies of the newly independent states was the erratic way new money was put into circulation. The inflationary policy was conducted mostly through credit expansion. The process by which individual enterprises converted their credit resources into cash was sporadic, unpredictable, and beyond the control of the government. It was accompanied by the uncontrolled and unpredictable flow of money from other states of the ruble zone. According to Patinkin (1989, p. 311), even during high inflation the economy can be reasonably stable if new injections of money are conducted at a constant rate. However, if time and amount of each new influx are unpredictable, consumers are likely to sharply increase demand for commodities in order to avoid the consequences of rising prices.

The erratic nature of inflation caused excessive demand for goods as well as for foreign currency. The increasing use of foreign currency (mostly US dollars and German marks) in internal transactions indicated that the domestic monetary systems were becoming irrelevant. This signaled the emergence of the phenomenon which Keynes described as "flight from the currency" (Keynes, 1936 (1964), p. 207) and which threatened not only the monetary system, but also the banking system. With monthly inflation steadily inching toward double-digit figures, the banking system in disarray due to the recklessly expanded credit, continuing shortages and mounting foreign debt (most of it to Russia for oil supplies), the economic situation demanded immediate action from decision-makers.

In the Baltics, the nationalist forces that came to power had to abandon the precepts of their original economic programs. The latter would entail increased redistributional activities of the government, while the disastrous state of their economies imposed limits on the state's ability to meet even its existing obligations. In Belarus, where economic challenges were the same as in the Baltics, the old elite had to abandon its attempts to exercise total control over the economy and took steps toward price liberalization. These measures alone, however, could not ensure the survival of the newly independent economies and prevent widespread social unrest as a direct consequence of the economic predicament.

Belarus and the Baltics: Similar Challenges, Different Responses

Monetary and budget crises of the magnitude described above indicated that economic disturbances were not confined to the financial system, but affected all aspects of economic processes. Consequently, governments of the newly independent states had to address immediate and basic economic problems, first and foremost, how to ensure an uninterrupted supply of basic goods and services. Of course, monetary adjustments were necessary, but they were considered only as long as they had a direct positive effect on the procurement and distribution of basic goods.

In the three Baltic states, the problem was approached as a short-term economic stabilization by means of trade liberalization. The logic of the first stage of the reforms was based on the recognition of one fact: the old enterprises which worked within the division of labor in the former USSR were unable to ensure a continuous supply of necessary commodities, and their immediate restructuring was impossible. Therefore, the state should reduce entry barriers for new economic agents, whose private activities would keep the economy alive. The emergence of viable economic entities on domestic markets would take time. Meanwhile, the foreign trade policy should be liberalized. Since foreign trade with the former Soviet republics was unlikely to produce positive results, efforts should be made to reorient foreign trade away from the former USSR. The key prerequisite to this move was the introduction of a stable domestic currency.

It is hard to describe this approach as a manifestation of liberal economic policy. Indeed, some of its elements very much resembled the Bolsheviks' new economic policy that was designed to employ foreign trade and market incentives for domestic private economic agents, combined with the introduction of a stable currency (intended mostly for foreign transactions). I am not implying that it was the "new economic policy" of Soviet Bolsheviks that inspired the Baltic reformers. Rather, this coincidence might indicate that in desperate economic situations the choice of instruments of economic recovery is not necessarily dictated by the ideological persuasions of reformers.

To facilitate the emergence of private economic agents, the necessary laws on rights of private ownership were passed in all three Baltic states in 1990 - 1992. However, by 1992 the private sector was still *in statu nascendi*, its development hampered by chaos in the banking and monetary system, as well as by the continuing domination of large industrial monopolies in the economy. The laws that liberalized foreign trade had been passed shortly after independence. At the same time, the Baltic states started to negotiate bilateral trade agreements with Western economies, seeking mutual preferential trade status and the removal of covert barriers to free exchanges. However, the results of these actions were delayed by the financial instability of the Baltic economies caused by their lack of control over their monetary systems.

Thus, the problem of monetary stability had a direct bearing upon the success of economic liberalization. Foreign trade with countries outside the former Soviet Union could not be conducted in non-cash Russian rubles, the only kind of currency the Baltic states could issue. Exit from the ruble zone and introduction of their own currency had become an urgent task. These actions would also benefit the incipient domestic private firms by easing access to credit and reducing uncertainty.

In 1992, Estonia, Latvia, and Lithuania had exited the ruble zone and started to introduce their own currencies. Lithuania introduced its provisional Talonas in May of 1992 and made it the sole legal tender by September of the same year, when all Russian rubles had been withdrawn from the circulation. The Latvian Rublis (also provisional) was introduced in May 1992 and became the sole legal tender two months later. The Estonian Kroon was the sole legal tender since its introduction in June 1992.

Both Latvia and Lithuania followed a two-step process in the introduction of their respective currencies. During the first stage, the goal was simply to introduce the national currency and establish control over monetary circulation. This stage did not include stabilization of the currency and its convertibility vis-a-vis the main Western currencies. Permanent, stable and convertible currencies were introduced in Lithuania and Latvia in 1993. Estonia introduced its Kroon as a permanent currency from the outset and ensured its stability and convertibilty by pegging its value to the German Mark and providing full backing by the country's gold and foreign currency reserves.

The introduction of national currencies, indeed, the creation of monetary systems from scratch, was a process of high technical complexity. The local experts, who had little or no knowledge of the modern monetary system, could not provide adequate expertise. Thus, technical assistance was actively sought in the West. In all three countries the assistance was provided by the World Bank, the International Monetary Fund, and the European Bank for Reconstruction and Development. In addition, Estonia received technical help from Finland and Sweden. This was facilitated by geographical proximity, historical and cultural ties and, in the case of Finland, the absence of the language barrier. Close cooperation of Estonian financial authorities and experts with their counterparts in Finland and Sweden (in fact a Swedish economist became Deputy Chairman of the Estonian National Bank) partly accounts for Estonia's success in the introduction of its currency.

While Western technical assistance to the Baltic states was indispensable for the establishment of adequate monetary and banking systems, it also contributed to a significant paradigm shift among the local economic experts and decision-makers. As the discussion in the previous chapter indicates, the former did not know much about the market, while the latter were ambivalent toward it. Now, they were easily persuaded by the Western advisers to adopt the radical "shock therapy" version of market reforms.

Several factors contributed to this paradigm shift. First, the Western experts possessed instrumental knowledge necessary to make viable economic decisions regarding highly complex technical issues. This gave credibility to their overall vision of economic transformation. Second, as Marie Lavigne (1995, p. 120) points out, the "shock therapy" model was the only approach to the problems of market reforms that was sufficiently detailed to provide a foundation for economic policy.[19] Third, since the radical approach was predominant in the World Bank and the IMF, these institutions actively used financial aid to force the countries in transition to comply with this approach.

Economic liberalization and monetary and financial stabilization per se do not constitute a radical "shock therapy" approach to economic reforms. In the Baltic states, as in many other countries in similarly dire circumstances, these measures were necessary to prevent a total economic breakdown. The overall package of the radical economic policy recommendations (of which they were only a part) can be described as radical for two reasons. As mentioned above, in the Baltic states immediately after independence monetary stabilization was not an end in itself, but a means to ensure the adequate supply of goods and services. However, economic stabilization typically anchors it to monetary indicators, such as inflation rates and money supply, that do not always reflect the situation on the developing market of goods and services. Moreover, the radical view of economic reform includes a rapid structural transformation and the privatization of large enterprises among the immediate tasks of economic transition policies. The feasibility of rapid and all-embracing structural reform in post-Soviet economies is highly questionable. And in fact, as will be discussed in detail in Chapter Four, a policy of rapid industrial restructuring and large-scale privatization proved to be less successful than expected by its advocates.

The introduction of new currencies in the Baltic states and their exit from the ruble zone had almost immediate positive effects. Inflation in all three countries was brought under control in 1993 and did not exceed ten per cent a month. Foreign trade was rapidly oriented away from the former USSR toward the West. A dramatic increase in foreign trade with countries outside the former Soviet Union coincided with the exit from the ruble zone. For Lithuania, share of former Soviet republics in total volume of exports fell from 95 percent in 1991 to 68 percent in 1993. In 1991 only 13 percent of Latvia's imports came from outside former Soviet Union, while in 1993 this figure was 31 percent. For Estonia share of non-Soviet countries in the total volume of imports increased even more dramatically, from 15 percent in 1991 to 76 percent in 1993 (Shen, 1994).

The first stage of the economic reforms provided the Baltic states with the necessary conditions for market development. They established stable monetary and banking systems, reduced the uncertainty inherent in hyperinflation, opened the incipient market to competition (both domestic and foreign). Most importantly, the economic collapse that seemed inevitable in the first year of independence had been successfully avoided.

In the long run, the reorientation of foreign trade should allow the Baltic states to drastically reduce, or even completely eliminate, their dependence on Russian oil supplies. The first steps toward this goal were made in 1992 and 1993, when each of the Baltic states started to build oil terminals that in future will be used to import oil by sea (Żidovicz, 1994, p. 73).

By comparison with the Baltics, Byelorussian foreign trade in the first years of independence still concentrated on the continuing exchange with the former Soviet republics. The volume of trade with countries outside the former Soviet Union dropped precipitously, almost by 40 percent, in 1991 and 1992 (State Statistical Committee of the Republic of Belarus, 1992, 1993). In relative terms, in 1993 countries outside the former Soviet Union accounted for 1.77% of the Byelorussian imports and 2.72% of exports (IMF, 1994a). In fact, the official Byelorussian statistical documents did not include the trade with the former Soviet republics in the category of foreign trade, suggesting the unwillingness of the Byelorussian authorities to part with the Soviet-style division of labor.

Belarus had chosen to remain in the ruble zone. It was confronted with the same problem as its Baltic neighbors: a chaotic and unpredictable nature of cash injections from other republics into the domestic economy. When it became clear that Russia would not coordinate its supply of rubles to Belarus with the Byelorussian needs, haphazard steps toward the introduction of the Byelorussian currency were finally taken. In May 1992 the Byelorussian ruble had been introduced into circulation. However, unlike the case of its Baltic counterparts, it was not intended as a permanent currency or even a step toward its eventual introduction. Officially defined as a "payment coupon", it was intended to supplement the Russian ruble during the temporary shortages of the latter on the Byelorussian territory (Council of Ministers of the Republic of Belarus, 1992). The new Byelorussian ruble was to be used only in cash transactions, with all non-cash operations still conducted in Russian rubles. As late as in the summer of 1994, the Byelorussian ruble had not yet become the sole legal tender in Belarus.

Price liberalization in Belarus started in 1991 and continued along the lines similar to the measures of the Polish communist government in the early

1980s. Prices were divided into three categories: "controlled", "limited", and "free". Prices in the first category were subsidized by the state. Both wholesale prices of oil and other energy sources delivered to enterprises and retail prices of heat and electricity used by household belonged to this category. "Limited" prices included those on products of the enterprises considered to occupy a monopolist position. These enterprises were allowed to raise prices up to a certain limit established by the authorities. Since most enterprises were monopolies in their respective fields, this measure amounted to the Soviet-style price control and was just as inefficient. The last category included all goods and services delivered to the non-state sector, as well as goods and services produced by it. This last feature of the Byelorussian price system discriminated against the few nascent non-state enterprises. Unable to compete with the subsidized state industries, private entrepreneurs were forced to concentrate on retail trade, where the cost of inputs did not present a major disadvantage.

Interenterprise arrears, that reached 126 billion rubles by July 1992, were annulled by the Byelorussian prime-minister, thus effectively adding this sum to the budget deficit (which translated itself into increased inflation). Negative-interest loans were routinely issued to the state industrial and agricultural enterprises. The Byelorussian authorities did not express their intention to bring interest rates closer to the rate of inflation. In fact, such attempts by the chairman of the Byelorussian National Bank were expressly prohibited by the government.

Relations of the Byelorussian authorities with the international economic agencies were the opposite of those in the Baltics. In my interview with the representative of the IMF in Belarus, he complained about the lack of training of the Byelorussian economic experts and decision-makers, as well as their lack of interest in training provided by the IMF. In his opinion, this was due to the lack of motivation. Local authorities did not want to learn about the market, because they did not want to move toward the market. Byelorussian government officials regarded the IMF only as a source of hard currency, not as a source of useful knowledge. This attitude was confirmed in my interviews with two medium-level officials in the Byelorussian Economic Ministry (the successor of the State Planning Committee). Both stated that the World Bank and the IMF are regarded by the Byelorussian decision-makers as a source of funds. Understanding that to receive these funds, they should exhibit a commitment to market reforms, Byelorussian authorities supply the World Bank and the IMF with information that may be interpreted as such a commitment. However, their actual decisions were decidedly anti-market.

Indeed, the Byelorussian leaders did not even try to conceal their unwillingness to conduct market reforms. For example, Prime Minister Kebich said in 1994 in his interview with a local newspaper: "we managed to stem the tide of reformist euphoria. Thanks to this, our people were not hungry, had their homes heated in the winter, produced goods, tilled the soil" (Kebich, 1994).

In the crisis, similar in its nature and magnitude to those experienced by the Baltic states, the strategy of the Byelorussian leadership was the opposite of the one adopted by its Baltic counterparts. Instead of monetary stabilization and economic liberalization, they opted for continuing subsidies and protection of the state enterprises. Their hope for revitalizing the economy lay in close relations with Russia. The gist of this strategy was clearly expressed by the Byelorussian Deputy Prime Minister Ivan Zalamai: "the economic and monetary union with Russia is absolutely necessary for the continuing operation of the existing enterprises. If the union is concluded, Belarus will be receiving steady supplies of raw materials, oil, and gas at the Russian domestic prices. Of course, monetary and credit decisions will be made in Moscow. However, Belarus must sacrifice some of its independence in order to save the economy. Proponents of the closer contacts with the West should realize that if these contacts materialize, we will have to buy everything at world market prices." (Zalamai, 1993). To explain the differences between the economic strategies of the Baltic and Byelorussian leaders, we should examine the interests of crucial social groups and the cognitive models of the ruling elites.

It would be incongruous to ask what social groups in post-Soviet countries benefitted the most from hyperinflation and other elements of the economic collapse. In the situation of total economic chaos only small number of profiteers have something to gain. The vast majority of the population loses, both in material and emotional terms. However, the losses are not evenly distributed among all social groups. Some stand to lose more than others, depending on their position in the political and economic system.[20]

In post-Soviet societies the workers and managers of large industrial enterprises were positioned better than any other social group to use inflationary processes for protection from imminent economic dislocation. Politically, their strong organization and the potentially dangerous conse-quences of unemployment gave them a strong bargaining position and allowed them to successfully demand expansion of cheap credit. Economi-cally, most enterprises were monopolist producers, which allowed them to rise prices. Thus, the situation had all the elements necessary for the classical cost inflation model as presented by Don Patinkin: strong labor combined with the state's declared policy of maintaining an absolutely continuous state of full employment (Patinkin, 1989, p. 310).

For the managers and employees of the state-controlled, mostly large, industrial enterprises, measures for economic stabilization and liberalization were detrimental, at least in the short run. They would expose these enterprises to the competition of foreign and then domestic producers. They would eliminate the soft budget constraints in their modified form of the negative interest rate credit and toleration of insolvency. This would effectively terminate the state policy of full employment and protection of all enterprise from bankruptcy. Of course, it would take some time actually to enforce the existing laws on bankruptcy, and a modicum of protection would be extended to the enterprises by any government willing to avoid an explosive growth in unemployment and related social problems. Still, even the relatively gradual encroachment of market forces on the comfortable monopolist positions of the state-controlled enterprises was not welcomed by their employees and managers.

In the Baltics, the industrial management well understood the full long-term implication of the introduction of the new currencies and the steps toward their convertibility against Western currencies (but not against the Russian ruble). Anatol Lieven quotes a Russian manager of an Estonian factory on the issue of the convertible Kroon: "If the Kroon really does become a hard currency, it could kill off most of the Estonian production, because the quality of Western production is so much higher than ours. At present, 90 percent of our trade is with the former Soviet Union. If we introduce the Kroon without full agreement on how to carry on payments, this will lead to practical blockade." (Lieven, 1993, p. 356). The resistance of the managers of the state-controlled enterprises in the Baltics to the introduction of national currencies is also pointed out by Shen (1994).

Industrial workers and managers in the Baltics, as well as in Belarus, constituted a formidable force, highly mobilized and capable of concerted and sustained actions. In the last years of the Soviet rule, as well as after the collapse of the Soviet Union, these groups successfully used their organization in the struggle for continuing government subsidies. For example, in the spring of 1992 the threat of industrial actions by workers' organizations in Eastern Estonia caused the government to provide subsidies, thus straining the financial system in the crucial time of the introduction of the Kroon. Similar demands were put forward during the strikes in Latvia and Lithuania.

However, for the managers and employees of industrial enterprises in the Baltics, the ability to force concessions from the government did not translate into the active participation in policy decision-making. This was due not to the lack of power, but rather to the specific pattern of mobilization and the image of workers' movements in the eyes of the new nationalist elites. In the last years of Soviet rule in the Baltics, industrial workers were mobilized around the Soviet imperial idea. Then, as an opposition to the fledgling nationalist movements, Moscow authorities together with the local hard-line Communists initiated the creation of mass anti-independence, pro-Soviet and pro-Communist movements. In Estonia, it was "The International Movement of Workers in the Estonian SSR"; in Latvia the similar movement was called the "International Front"; in Lithuania it was known as "Unity".

These movements were centered around large industrial enterprises and quickly acquired a truly mass character. Their organizers capitalized on the ethnic composition of the industrial workforce. In Latvia, where the share of non-indigenous population in industrial employment was the largest of the three Baltic states, the Russian-speaking workers constituted 59.4 percent of the total number of industrial workers (Karklins, 1994, p. 133). The figure was similar in Estonia, where the Russian-speaking population was concentrated in industrial centers in the East of the country. Fears of the non-indigenous population, whose future status in the independent Baltic states was unclear and who often distrusted the nationalist leaders, proved a fertile ground for the cultivation of Soviet loyalism, especially when combined with economic considerations. All these movements proclaimed their loyalty to the Soviet Union and opposed any action of the nationalist movements by staging mass demonstrations and industrial actions. Two examples may serve to illustrate the agenda of these "international workers' movements". In 1989, a wave of mass demonstrations and strikes was organized by them in Lithuania, Latvia, and Estonia to protest against measures to make indigenous languages official (Nahaylo and Swoboda, 1990, p. 319). In August 1989, the Estonian International Movement organized a general strike to stop the attempts by the Estonian authorities to remove enterprises from the control of Moscow (Lieven, 1994, p. 193). Both these actions involved tens of thousands of participants.

The workers' movements in the Baltics actively participated in the 1990 elections in local legislative bodies. They supported candidates who shared their agenda (often, but not necessarily, also supported by the official Communist establishment) and who, when elected, formed parliamentary factions that were not only pro-worker, but also pro-Soviet. After their active support of the Soviet military actions in Lithuania and Latvia in the winter of 1991, as well as the August 1991 coup, deputies belonging to these factions had their mandates annulled. Thus, when the crucial first steps of economic reforms were taken, industrial workers and management did not have political representation.

The actions of the workers' movements prior to independence, as well as the openly pro-Soviet stance of the parliamentary factions supported by these movements, contributed to the image of large industrial enterprises as a potential pro-Russian "fifth column". Thus, they were regarded by the decision-makers not as legitimate participants in the reform process, but as an alien force to be reckoned, but not cooperated with. The fact that in 1992 in all three Baltic states positions crucial for the formulation of reform policies (Prime Ministers, their deputies, and chairpersons of national banks) were held by staunch nationalists, served further to reinforce this attitude. The exclusion of the industrial workers and managers from political discourse regarding specific elements of the reforms made it easier for the reformers in the Baltics to introduce stabilization measures in compliance with the requirements of the World Bank and the IMF. Many industrial managers well understood the long-term consequences of such policies. However, the highly complex technical nature of the issues involved made it difficult to mobilize workers against them.

In Belarus, large industrial enterprises had support not only in legislation, where more than 30% of deputies were managers of state-controlled firms, but also in the executive branch of government. In my interviews with five high-ranking members of the Byelorussian government apparatus (three directors of departments in the Ministry of Economics, the Deputy Finance Minister, and the Chair of the State Anti-Monopoly Committee) all five interviewees pointed to very close connections between directors of industrial enterprises and the actual decision-makers in the government. The latter, confined mostly to the prime minister and his deputies, would make their decisions on economic policies only after consultations with the former. Thus, unlike their Baltic counterparts, Byelorussian industrial managers were actively participating in detailed analysis and in the formulation of economic policy decisions. Their control of the legislature ensured that only those laws that satisfied them would pass.

The above comparison of the influence of industrial managers and workers on the reform process in Belarus and the Baltics might seem to fall into Olson's model of "distributional coalitions" and their role in the economic progress of societies (Olson, 1982). Indeed, in his later work (1993) he attributed both the Soviet economic collapse and post-Soviet stagnation to the negative influence of such coalitions. In our case, the first stage of economic reforms succeeded in the Baltics because "distributional coalitions" were excluded from decision-making, while in Belarus reforms faltered because these coalitions retained their influence. However, if we consider the causes of the different influence of large industrial enterprises in Belarus as compared to the Baltics, the applicability of Olson's model becomes less obvious. The power of industrial enterprises in the Baltics was equal to or even greater than that of their counterparts in Belarus. The main reason for their exclusion from decision-making was the value-pattern of the nationalist ruling elites. In Belarus, on the other hand, the ruling elite's attitude toward industrial enterprises was universally positive. Thus, the exclusion of "distributional coalitions" in the Baltics and their participation in decision-making in Belarus were due to factors that are beyond the frame of reference adopted by Olson and rational action theory in general.

The first stage of economic reforms in the Baltics had been much more successful than in Belarus. This difference was to a large extent due to the value-system of the ruling elites, particularly their attitudes toward Russia, as well as the place of the existing industrial structure in the legitimation pattern. In the chapter that follows we discuss the next stage of economic reforms.

Notes

1   Party control over the discussion was confined to keeping the most radical reform blueprints, that advocated a rapid transition to capitalism, outside the official debate.

2   One should remember that in Soviet-type economies overt inflation is always accompanied by latent inflation that reveals itself mostly as a shortage of consumer goods and services. This latter type of inflation is almost impossible to precisely measure. However, there are indications that in Poland in the 1980s it was quite high.

3   According to a survey conducted in 1989 among the university students in the Soviet republics, only 4% of the Balts regarded the October Revolution as an event that positively influenced their countries, while among the Russians this figure was 46%. Attitudes toward the victory in Great Patriotic War were similarly distributed (Novikova et al., 1989).

4   For a vivid description of the "national Communist" aspects of the Baltic leadership in the 1950s and 1960s see for example: Anatol Lieven, *The Baltic Revolution*. New Haven: Yale University Press, 1993, pp. 94-98.

5   In fact, all major nationalist newspapers in Lithuania, Latvia, and Estonia, used printing facilities of official Communist periodicals.

6   For more information on this subject, see for example: Ivanov, M. 'The Byelorussians of Eastern Poland under Soviet Occupation, 1939-1941', in: *The Soviet Takeover of the*

Polish Eastern Provinces, 1939-41, ed. by Keith Sword, New York, St. Martin's Press, 1991, pp. 253-254.

7   In 1925, a member of the Polish government predicted that "in ten years you will not find, even with a candle, a single Byelorussian in Poland." (Lubachko, 1972, p. 135.)

8   Relations between the Byelorussian national intelligentsia and the Polish authorities were quite complex. The latter conducted a policy of Polonization and at the same time allowed to create various organizations promoting Byelorussian cause. J. Gross even states that "despite the injustices..., the material, spiritual, and political life of the national minorities in interwar Poland was richer and more complex than ever before or after." (Gross, 1988, p. 6.)

9   For more details see Tsvikevich, A. 1927, pp. 23-38.

10   On the Soviet occupation of Western Byelorussia see: Gross, 1988, p. 29.

11   For more detailed information about Byelorussia under the German occupation, see: Dallin, 1957, pp. 199-215; Lubachko, 1972, pp. 146-157; Vakar, 1956, pp. 170-194.

12   A cleavage between rural (traditional and predominantly Byelorussian) and urban (international with very strong Russian orientation) culture had been a popular topic of discourse in the Byelorussian academic and literary circles; among the most detailed accounts of this controversy see, for example: Antsipenka, 1992.

13   M. Urban (1989, p. 140) suggests that the central authorities actively participated in this leadership change.

14   Estimates were made using data of the official Soviet statistical agency, whose figures regarding interrepublican exchange always overestimated the flow of raw materials and energy sources and underestimated the value of manufactured goods.

15   Russia's strong position in trade with the former republics should not be confused with position of individual Russian enterprises. Some of them depended on supplies from the Baltics and Belarus and were suffering from disruption of supplies just as their counterparts there.

16   More precisely, it was the share of profit above the centrally established amount needed for the internal use by the enterprise. In the Soviet accounting practice it was called "a free remainder of the profit subject to transfer to the budget". While the all-Union enterprises transferred it to the central budget, profit of republican enterprises served as a source of revenue for republican budgets.

17   Turnover tax was a uniquely Soviet economic phenomenon. Its closest analogue would be excise tax. Turnover tax was imposed on most consumer goods. Each group of commodities was taxed at its own rate. Unlike sales tax, it was collected from producers and, in some cases, wholesale distributors, rather than retailers. Unlike VAT, it was calculated on the basis of the total cost of the unit of a taxed commodity (and not only its added value).

18   Because of the underdeveloped banking system in the former Soviet Union, all transactions by individual consumers had to be conducted in cash.

19   "There was no theory of gradualism. While shock therapy approaches were widely advocated for policy-making, there has been no *specific* plea for gradualism, only recommendations to the effect of softening the initial shocks whenever there had been an "overshooting"" (Lavigne, 1995, p. 120, italics added).

20   "A change in the value of money, that is to say in the level of prices, is important to Society only in so far as its incidence is unequal. Such changes have produced in the past, and are producing now, the vastest social consequences, because, as we all know, when the value of money changes, it does not change equally for all persons or for all purposes.

A man's receipts and his outgoings are not all modified in one uniform proportion. Thus a change in prices and rewards, as measured in money, generally affects different classes unequally, transfers wealth from one to another, bestows affluence here and embarrassment there, and redistributes Fortune's favors so as to frustrate design and disappoint expectation" (Keynes, 1923 (1963), pp. 80-81).

4 Early Privatization: Expectations and Realities

The collapse of the Soviet system revealed not only the inadequacy of its socio-economic and political structures but also the lack of suitable explanatory frameworks. This applies both to the developments preceding the collapse and the post-Soviet transformations. A sort of intellectual vacuum in this field prevailed both within former Soviet academic communities and among their counterparts in the West. Since the vacuum coincided with dire circumstances in the unravelling Communist economies, it was only natural that many outside observers were eager to combine theoretical explanation and practical advice. However, these combinations often founded strong practical recommendations on theories that have not been tested in conditions approaching those of post-Communist economies and societies.

One of the theories developed without a specific reference to the post-Communist transition process and not intended as a foundation of policy decision-making, but nonetheless used as a tool for policy formulation, was the property rights approach to economic efficiency. The authors of the original property rights theory never regarded the system of property rights as something easily changeable by policy decisions. However, as we shall see in the discussion that follows, their theory was interpreted in a way that made it a foundation for economic reform policies.

Up to now, studies of post-Soviet economic transformations as well as recommendations for policy decisions concentrated almost exclusively on rapid government-conducted changes of the property system. The goal of the government was to achieve a short-term economic equilibrium, create a new system of property rights, and then to assume a purely laissez-faire position in economic matters. The view of the government-originated system of private property rights as the main vehicle toward a market economy borrows its theoretical premises from the property rights approach to economic efficiency.

On a more abstract level, relations between power and efficiency within complex organization were discussed by Armen Alchian (1950). Later, studies in economic history by Douglas North (1971, 1981) and comparative economics by Svetozar Pejovich (1969) introduced the main elements of property rights theory. These authors, each choosing his own approach to the problem and method of its investigation, convincingly argued that there is a correlation between institutional arrangements and economic efficiency.

At the start of the post-Communist economic transformations, the property rights perspective was the only theoretical paradigm that could directly address the problems of systemic economic transformation. Another paradigm applied to post-Communist developments, namely neo-classical economics, defined the desirable state of affairs (the free market) but did not provide specific suggestions as to how it could be achieved. At the same time, in the context of post-Communist reforms these two paradigms became compatible and mutually complementing as two parts of a single transition design.

Since in the neo-liberal economic paradigm the pure and free market is regarded as the most efficient of all economic systems, a suboptimal efficiency is ascribed to non-economic forces interfering with the workings of the spontaneous market mechanism. The latter point is elaborated in property rights theory. Alchian maintains that there is a direct link between economic efficiency and political arrangements. In his view, if an economic system operates below its optimal level of efficiency, this is due to political constraints blocking rearrangements of the existing property rights structure (Alchian, 1950). North establishes historical relations between the political power of the state and the property rights system. According to him, the power of the state influences the system of property rights in the following ways. First, states specify fundamental rules of the property rights structure. Second, states provide a set of goods and services designed to lower transaction costs (thus indirectly strengthening the existing property rights system) (North, 1979). Pejovich, in his latest work, provides a detailed account of the mechanism whereby the property rights system, supported by political power arrangements, influences the performance of various economic systems (Pejovich, 1995). In the works of the reform-oriented East European economists (e.g. Winiecki, 1990; 1995), as well as Western observers (e.g. Cooter, 1991; Newberry, 1992), the correlation between property rights and economic efficiency, as well as the role the state plays in maintaining a system of property rights already in existence, was taken to imply that changing the existing property rights by governmental decree would immediately expose enterprises to market forces, which in turn would facilitate the overall efficiency of the whole economic system. An example of such optimistic predictions based on the property rights approach can be found in works of Jan Winiecki (1990). He maintained that there will be no opposition to privatization among the industrial blue-collar workers because the privatized enterprises will immediately increase their efficiency and this increase will have a speedy and tangible positive impact on the workers' living conditions.

The above view was based on what Winiecki called "the methodological directive" which, in accordance with theoretical postulates developed by Alchian and North, pointed to political constraints as the main obstacle to the efficiency-increasing change (Winiecki, 1990, p. 10). In this view political changes are necessary and sufficient for rapid marketization of the former state enterprises, which in turn would lead to a capitalist market economy. Winiecki discounts the emergence of small private enterprises as a viable path toward the capitalist market. He maintains that without prior mass privatization of large state-owned enterprises the emerging private business will be "contaminated" by the dominant property rights structure, and its expansion will not bring tangible benefits for the process of economic transformation (Winiecki, 1990, p. 12). The implicit corollary is that this contamination can be avoided by rapid state actions directed toward creation of a new structure of property rights. In this he is echoed by David Newbery who asserts that "the rapid, unambiguous creation and defense of private property" is a viable task for the state apparatus (Newbery, 1992, p. 217). Interestingly enough, the author does not distinguish between such different tasks as defense and creation of private property. Thus, even though the basic premises of the property rights approach were adopted by proponents of rapid privatization, the approach was substantially modified. Now, from a descriptive theory based on verifiable information pertaining to long-term socio-economic development, it became an analytical tool for activist economic policy of relatively short-term reforms.

Proponents of the property rights approach to post-Communist economic transformation interpreted the inefficiency of state-owned enterprises as a manifestation of a purely technical problem rooted primarily in the asymmetry of information available to various economic actors. Institutional economics sees the cause of this problem in the "principal - agent" relationship. This relationship exists where one party (the agent) is supposed to act in the interests of another party (the principal). The problem arises under the following two conditions: first, the agent's objectives differ from those of the principal and second, the former possesses more information about actual performance of the economic unit entrusted to him/her than is available to the latter. In Soviet-type economies, where the state was the principal and enterprise managers, agents, the above conditions did exist. They were recognized as a major cause of low economic performance of centrally planned economic structures. However, some researchers cautioned against the tendency to ascribe a purely informational nature to the "principal-agent" problem in STEs (Kornai, 1992, p. 371). Others pointed out that this problem exists for privately owned enterprises with dispersed ownership and not only for publicly owned economic units (George, 1991, p. 170; Milor, 1994, pp. 6-7). However, the problem was particularly acute in STEs and privatization of state-owned enterprises was considered a solution whereby the agent receives more incentives for efficient performance than under the state ownership.

Despite the predominance of the above approach to post-Communist economic reforms in academic discourse and its support and acceptance as a foundation for economic policies by international economic agencies, it was by no means universally shared.

Mancur Olson pointed out that the term "privatization" as applied to post-Soviet societies is ambiguous and "does not have the clear meaning that it has in the mature democracies of the West" (Olson, 1992, p. 71). Kazimierz Poznanski, even though he accepts the main postulates of the property rights theory, expressed serious doubts about the effectiveness of economic reforms based on this approach (Poznanski, 1992). Peter Murrell is among the most vocal critics of the activist interpretations of the property rights theory. As early as 1992 he warned that privatizing state-owned enterprises is bound to be a long and costly process and that reformers' energy would be more effectively applied to facilitating the growth of the new private sector (Murrell, 1992, p. 52).

The cautious (and, as it proved to be, realistic) approach to economic transformation was not adopted as a foundation for reform policies. A combination of neo-liberal economics and property rights theory remained the dominant intellectual trend among both Western advisors and local decision-makers. The reasons for that were not exclusively of an economic nature. As Marie Lavigne suggests, the policy of rapid large-scale privatization served as an expression of political commitment to a free market economy (Lavigne, 1995, p. 119). Similar views are expressed by Andreas Pickel who regards neo-liberal economics as a foundation of an official post-Communist ideology rather than a realistic economic program (Pickel, 1995, p. 373).

Now, nine years after the first laws on privatization had been passed in post-Soviet countries, it is possible to make some tentative assessments of this much discussed and apparently promising form of economic restructuring. In this chapter I continue the comparative analysis of transitional processes in Poland and four former Soviet republics: Belarus, Lithuania, Latvia, and Estonia.

Poland, Belarus and the Baltic states shared the same network of institutions of the Soviet-type economy and therefore were roughly equally distant from the developed capitalist market economy as late as 1989-90. However, by 1994 it had become apparent that market development in Poland and the three Baltic states has gained momentum and become irreversible. At the same time, in Belarus market transformations were going slowly and in the summer of 1994 the policy of market reforms had been abandoned by the new Byelorussian government. According to the European Bank for Reconstruction and Development, in 1994 55 percent of Poland's GNP was produced in the private sector; the figure was the same for Latvia and Estonia, and slightly lower for Lithuania (50 percent). At the same time, in Belarus only 15 percent of GNP was produced in the private sector (EBRD, 1994). Thus, if Poland and the three Baltic states by 1994 had approached a "critical mass" of irreversible market transformations, which since proved to be immune to the vagaries of post-Soviet political life, the situation in Belarus allowed to keep its economy on the old Soviet track. Recent reports indicate that these two divergent trends continue. According to the EBRD Transition Report, Poland and the three Baltic states are currently experiencing economic growth driven primarily by private enterprises, while Belarus have taken steps backwards from already low level of reforms (EBRD, 1997).

Even allowing for the short time involved, the differences are so profound, they cannot be regarded merely as matters of degree or idiosyncratic peculiarities of various economic reforms. Is this difference due to successful mass privatization programs in Poland and the Baltics as opposed to the failure of Byelorussian reformers to privatize their large enterprises? If this were true, then mass privatization could be regarded as the most promising way toward the market. However, at this point this contention is by no means proven, and the discussion that follows is intended to clarify the issue.

Despite the original intentions of reformers, political considerations were introduced in market reform design from the outset and often prevailed over economic rationality. The predominance of political motives manifests itself in many ways and at every stage of privatization, from the initial valuation of assets to managing privatized enterprises.

In most countries the state-owned assets singled out for privatization were evaluated by government agencies, with little regard for possible market demand (or in close cooperation with large investment funds closely related to the state apparatus). A significant number of shares was given to the workers and managers of privatized enterprises. In some countries (for example, Russia) privatization amounted to a transfer of controlling stakes of shares to insiders as well as to other enterprises, banks and investment funds directly or indirectly controlled by the state (Nellis, 1994). Ira Lieberman observed that as a result of mass privatization programs, state institutions (such as state property funds and committees) invariably end up being the largest single shareholders in the country (1995, p. 15) due to the accumulation of unsold shares. This is true for almost all former Soviet-type economies, regardless of the government's commitment to introduce market reforms.

Even in Poland, where the government has not lacked resolve in conducting consistent market reforms (and where socio-political conditions for transition are more favorable than in most other post-Communist countries), the privatization program has hardly been a success. Initially announced in 1990, it targeted 500 enterprises for privatization. However, in 1992, the target figure had shrunk to 200 enterprises (out of a total of 8,000). Without achieving even this reduced goal, the program has been revised and modified several times (Levitas, 1994, pp. 104-105). The next version of the program was based on the Law of National Investment Funds and Their Privatization of April 30, 1993 (Jerzy Thieme, 1995, p. 39). But this version too from the start encountered significant difficulties and eventually was lost in a quagmire of political debates (Swiatkowski, 1994). Only by the Summer of 1997 did this program achieve tangible results by offering on the Warsaw stock exchange shares of mutual funds representing about 500 medium size industrial enterprises that accounted for approximately 10% of Poland's industrial output (*Wall Street Journal*, June 13, 1997). This success has been long in coming, thus illustrating that even modest changes of the property structure of the existing assets take much longer than was initially predicted.

At the beginning, the mass privatization program in Lithuania seemed to be more successful than its Polish counterpart. By 1994, more than half of the former state enterprises had been privatized, amounting to 46 percent of the total number of enterprises in industry, 39 percent in transportation, 55 percent in trade and commerce, and 77 percent in services. As in Poland, the initial goal of the reformers was to achieve greater economic efficiency through the privatization of state-owned assets. This aim was reflected in its first version of the mass privatization program, according to which two thirds of the state-owned property was to be privatized within two to three years; an autonomous structure of privatization bodies was to be created to assure their independence from political pressures; and employees of state-owned enterprises being privatized were allowed to buy up to ten per cent of the shares of the enterprise on favorable terms without any additional privileges (Simenas, 1995, p. 108).

From the outset the Lithuanian mass privatization program was designed to create a completely new structure of property rights. Upon its completion, the private sector, non-existent for almost five decades of Soviet rule, was to be predominant in industry, construction, trade, services and agriculture, with transportation and utilities remaining in the public sector. It is interesting to note that by 1994 the share of privatized enterprises in transportation and utilities was quite significant (39 and 27 per cent respectively). This went beyond the targets of the original version of the program. Does it indicate that later versions were becoming more economically radical?

Actually, the opposite was the case. Despite visible successes of the mass privatization program in its early stages, it has been significantly changed. In 1993 the Lithuanian parliament (Sejmas) amended the Law on privatization to give employees the right to purchase up to 50 per cent of shares at the nominal value. The employees were allowed to use profit reserves of the enterprise to purchase shares. With the market price of shares often being much higher than their nominal value, this amendment was clearly motivated by political rather than economic considerations. Other modifications of the programs included the introduction of closed auctions and subscriptions for shares. In addition, the role of supposedly autonomous privatization agencies was weakened by the increased influence of various enterprises and ministries in the privatization policy process. These measures favored the insiders and precluded the most efficient way of privatization. With privatization essentially changing its nature and becoming the process of giving state-owned assets away to management and workers, the list of enterprises targeted for this kind of privatization has been expanded to include those enterprises in utilities and transportation which initially were intended to remain public property. Thus, given the nature of mass privatization in Lithuania, we have to exercise caution when assessing its progress since many enterprises labeled as privatized had in fact been jointly owned by the employees and the state with very little influence from outside investors.

The Latvian mass privatization program, despite ambitious plans to privatize around 700 medium and large-scale enterprises by the end of 1993, came to an almost complete halt, with only 85 enterprises privatized by April 1994. However, the privatization of small enterprises proceeded at a much faster pace. By April 1994 two thirds of such enterprises had been sold to private owners (IMF, 1994b).

A similar situation emerged in Estonia, where more than 90 percent of small enterprises in retail trade and 80 percent in services had been privatized by the end of 1993. At the same time, privatization of medium and large-scale enterprises has not been so successful, with only 50 companies having been sold. It is important to note that the Estonian reformers, not unlike their Polish counterparts, have tried to conduct their privatization program by using open tenders where all potential investors (both foreign and domestic) can take part. Later, a public sale of shares was increasingly used as a method of privatization, although without much success (IMF, 1994a).

On the surface, both the program and progress of the mass privatization in Belarus did not seem to differ from those in Lithuania, Latvia, or Poland. The legal framework created by 1993 allowed both large- and small-scale enterprises to be privatized. The main privatization agency -- the Ministry of State Property and Privatization -- was in a position to make decisions and determine privatization policies independently of other ministries. Judging by the sheer numbers of the privatized enterprises, privatization in Belarus has been moderately successful compared, for example, to Poland or Latvia. Privatization started in 1991 and by the end of 1992 more than 270 enterprises were leased to private entities. In 1993, after the Law on Privatization of State Property and the Law on Privatization Vouchers had been approved, the privatization process entered a new phase. According to the Ministry of Management of State Property and Privatization of the Republic of Belarus, mass privatization of state-owned enterprises began in June 1993 and by the end of that year 140 enterprises had been privatized. By May 1994 another 73 enterprises were privatized, largely through the conversion of state-owned enterprises into joint-stock companies. As in other countries, only few enterprises have been sold through auctions and tenders (eighteen in 1993, and only four in the first half of 1994).

The results of privatization seem to indicate that by 1994 in Belarus some progress had been made in changing forms of property and that the country has made not insignificant strides toward a market economy. In fact, if we consider progress of privatization an important criterion of the success of market-oriented reforms, Belarus in 1994 could be seen as being in a better position than Poland or Latvia where mass privatization then had not yet started in earnest. However, these numbers are misleading.

If judged by their respective shares of GNP produced by the private sector, Belarus with 15 percent was in its market transition far behind Poland and the three Baltic states, where this share was in each case in excess of 50 percent. This comparison clearly puts in doubt the assumed correlation between a success of the mass privatization and progress toward a market economy. Now two questions have to be answered. The first: what causes a mass privatization program to stall (as in Poland) or change its nature (as in Lithuania)? The second question: if the progress of mass privatization does not serve as an indicator of the emergence of market economy, what factors can account for variations in the success of market reforms?

Attempting to answer the first question, we will analyze the Polish approach to privatization as well as the socio-political forces that shaped its decision-making. Poland was the first Communist country in Eastern Europe to start a slow but tumultuous process of moving away from the social, political, and economic structures of a Soviet-type regime. Also, the privatization program in Poland provides insights into the programs in other post-Soviet countries because they contain similar features. These features include, first, attempts by at least the more serious reformers to follow examples of Western privatization processes and generally to build their programs explicitly on theoretical foundations from neo-classical economics (in its Thatcherite version). It also reflects the desire of the general public for social justice and equality in the redistribution of state-owned assets; and in addition it reflects the power of organized workers who (together with managers of enterprises) try to maintain their job and income security.

The first feature is probably more salient in Poland due to the closer affiliation of its intellectual elite with the Western intellectual tradition. This is demonstrated by every aspect of its program, as in its attempts to use public offerings on the Warsaw stock exchange as a major way to privatize a substantial portion of state-owned assets, thus replicating the principal method of privatization in Great Britain in the '80s. But this strategy resulted in a very slow progress. Twenty four public offerings had been made by August 1994 and an additional sixty enterprises had been sold to foreign investors (Swiatkowski, 1994). The most recent success in selling the assets of 500 medium-size enterprises in the Summer of 1997 has been six years in the making, far exceeding the time intended by the reformers.

Attempts to accommodate the public desire for equal distribution of state-owned assets are common for all privatization programs. This desire was enhanced by public outrage against so called "nomenklatura privatization" in the early '90s which resulted in transfers of property rights to former party officials and high-ranking executives. All privatization programs included various forms of voucher privatization, in which a voucher guaranteed its owner the right to a specific share of the state-owned property. In some countries, vouchers were tradeable for shares of the privatized enterprises offered in public auctions (e.g., in Russia, the Czech Republic, or Lithuania). In other countries privatization laws required a mandatory placement of individual vouchers in specially designed investment funds. In the latter case, owners did not have the option of trading their vouchers directly for shares of enterprises, as an individual voucher-holder may choose to do (e.g., in Poland). The value of vouchers allocated to each citizen generally varied according to his/her age or number of years at work. This may provide some semblance of social justice, but it works against economic efficiency since a large percentage of shares was concentrated in the hands of elderly people who are unlikely to engage in active (and potentially risky) investment activities. In Poland, the voucher privatization scheme was debated since the first version of mass privatization program was announced (in 1990), but little of a practical nature has been done to implement it. Four years later, in 1994, plans to distribute vouchers among 27 million adult Polish citizens were still under discussion (Swiatkowski, 1994).

In addition, Polish privatization programs have taken into account the substantial power of workers and managers of state-owned enterprises, and made some concessions to their demands. All privatization programs have distributed major shares of the privatized enterprises to their workers and managers. In Poland this figure rose from 10 per cent in the first version of the program to 15 percent in 1994 (Winiecki, 1995, p. 53). In many cases, this effectively gave control of the enterprises to the employees. The programs contained an element which has given employees complete control over some enterprises: a provision for lease or sale of an enterprise to its employees through a so called enterprise-led liquidation procedure. In 1991, 415 firms had been privatized using this procedure (Levitas, 1994, p. 107) and by 1994 the figure increased to 1000 enterprises (Thieme, 1995, p. 40).

Workers also won the right to retain their job and income security by avoiding privatization entirely, while state control over enterprises was significantly reduced. In 1994, more than one half of the Polish labor force still worked in state-owned enterprises (Thieme, 1995, p. 47). Workers continued to reap the benefits provided by the essentially monopolistic position of their enterprises while no longer having to carry the burden of detailed centralized planning. Since the power of organized and mobilized workers in Poland became an important factor in the socio-political process during the rise of Solidarity, they remained in a good bargaining position vis-a-vis the state apparatus and the group of market-oriented reformers; thus they were able successfully to resist those reforms which they saw as threatening their well-being. Privatization regarded by the reformers as an exclusively economic process was hampered by political counterforces.

When some authors write about privatization as a means of depoliticization of an economic system (e.g. Boycko, Shleifer, and Vishny, 1995, p. 155) they seem to miss the fact that mass privatization is itself an eminently political process. In the example of Polish mass privatization (or lack thereof), we can clearly distinguish at least three political forces, each with its own interests and aspirations, whose interaction shaped both the plans of privatization and their actual implementation.

Before the collapse of Communist regime in Poland, proponents of radical economic reforms were convinced that the only major obstacle to successful economic reforms was the Communist ruling elite (Winiecki, 1990). When the most active and powerful resistance to the reforms came from the organized workers, the reformers tried to explain it by the survival of former Communists in high positions in the political system (Winiecki, 1995, p. 56). They chose to ignore the fact that the industrial workers proved to be an important group in a position to affect the outcome of mass privatization. Transfer of property rights to employees of state enterprises, through the process of so called "enterprise-led liquidation", has been the most successful element of the Polish mass privatization program. In other countries, workers receive significant percentages of shares in the privatized enterprises. Even though the reformers consider this an economically inefficient solution, industrial workers possess enough power to have their demands accommodated.

In Poland, more than 1000 firms were transferred to employees by 1994, compared to less than one hundred enterprises privatized through public offerings on the Warsaw stock exchange during the same period (Thieme, 1995, p. 40). In Russia, workers can choose between receiving 25 percent of the shares of an enterprise free and an additional 10 percent at a 30 percent discount, or acquiring together with management 51 percent of the equity at prices well below the market value of the assets. About 20 per cent of shares remains in the government's hands (Boycko, Shleifer, Vishny, 1995, p. 160). In Lithuania, the companies privatized from September 1991 to early 1992 have up to 20 per cent combined employees/management ownership and up to 50 per cent owned by the government (Semeta, 1995, p. 121). It is clear that workers (or workers and the government) actually exercise property rights, whereas other investors either do not exist or are small and dispersed and thus unable to effectively influence decision-making. Thus, the "principal-agent" problem in its classical form remained even after the property right system had been modified.

Since the workers (together with management and the government) are the ones who effectively exercise property rights, their interests are likely to be predominant in the restructuring of privatized enterprises. Personnel of any organization are interested in two things: collectively, in the organization's survival, and individually, in receiving the highest possible rewards. Survival of industrial enterprises is tacitly guaranteed by the state which remains a major stockholder and is very reluctant to implement the existing bankruptcy laws. Stable (if not very high) income is guaranteed by the monopolistic position of virtually every enterprise in an environment characterized by high demand and low supply of even the most basic goods and services.

As we shall see in the discussion that follows, attempts to undermine the monopolist positions of large enterprises are ineffective. Experience with workers' self-management in the former Yugoslavia indicates that workers are very reluctant to use profits for capital investment and restructuring of their enterprises.[1] Instead, they try to spend all profits on wages, bonuses, facilities providing services exclusively to the employees of a given enterprise (day care centers, health care facilities, etc), and other modes of personal consumption.

One should keep in mind that Svetozar Pejovich based his conclusions about workers' behavior solely on the analysis of the collectively owned Yugoslav enterprises. There had been no alternative forms of ownership in the Yugoslav industry, and the collectively owned enterprises enjoyed soft budget constraints tolerated by the government. I think that these two factors contributed to Pejovich's conclusion at least as much as the workers' collective ownership. In the absence of soft budget constraints and in a competitive environment, enterprises collectively owned by their employees do not have inherent features leading to inefficient investment decisions. However, the situation in the former Soviet economies is marked by the lack of competition and continuing support of inefficient enterprises by the state. Therefore, there is no evidence suggesting that the behavior of workers in privatized enterprises in Poland, the Baltic states, Russia, Belarus, or any other post-Soviet country is likely to be different from that of those counterparts in the former Yugoslavia.

Workers of the ostensibly privatized enterprises effectively under employees' control are likely to behave contrary to rational investment strategies until the emergence of viable competition. To this we can add that workers and management of the enterprises still officially owned by the state are effectively in control of their enterprises and have no interest in changing the situation. The following description of how a state-controlled enterprise operates in a post-Soviet economy is based on interviews with the head of the department of prices at the Minsk meat packing plant and two heads of departments at Belarus' s Ministry of the Economy.

State-owned enterprises in Belarus do not receive production plans from their ministries as they used to in pre-reform Soviet economy. Essentially, they are permitted to produce what they choose. Some enterprises, particularly in the food-processing industry, receive a state order for their products which means that the state guarantees that it will buy a particular amount of these products. In most cases this guarantee covers close to ninety percent of the total output. If an enterprise is considered a monopoly and if it receives a state order for some of its products, prices of these products are established by the state. However, the enterprise has a strong bargaining position in negotiating prices with the state agencies, a process that is repeated as prices go up. The state controls prices by establishing the maximum profit margin (five percent in food processing industry, significantly higher for other industries). However, production costs are not controlled by the state. If an enterprise points to rising costs as the main factor in its price increase, it is always permitted to increase the price. The enterprise's benefits from this arrangement are twofold: an uncontrolled increase in production costs means an uncontrolled growth of wages and increased costs, together with fixed profit margins, increase the absolute amount of profit. If enterprise is not satisfied with a price, it can always negotiate higher prices directly with buyers (in the case of the food processing industry, retail trade outlets). In such negotiations an enterprise has the advantage of its monopolist position.

In the food processing industry, local authorities exercise more effective control over enterprises than the state agencies. The power of local councils over enterprises in this case is based on the fact that they buy most of their products. Individual buyers (retail trade and catering enterprises), both state-owned and private, have to obtain a quota from the local council that entitles them to purchase a particular amount of foodstuffs. Local councils have a right to assign a mandatory product mix to each food processing enterprise oriented to the local market. Thus, local councils effectively control retail trade and catering by increasing or lowering purchasing quotas as well as food processing enterprises in the region (both through quotas and mandatory product mix).

In industries other than food processing, enterprises do not have a buyer (or buyers) who will purchase a guaranteed amount of their products. As in a market economy, they have to find buyers without help from the state. This makes such enterprises even less dependent on their ministries. Since the latter have a right to grant or withhold export licenses, they still possess some power vis-a-vis the subordinate enterprises. Export licenses open extremely lucrative opportunities because they can cover not only finished goods produced by enterprises but virtually every asset. This may include, for example, raw materials obtained from other CIS countries (Belarus itself is not rich in natural resources) and sold abroad at much higher prices. Theoretically, an enterprise can obtain an export license for products unrelated to its production activities. Among the most popular items being exported are non-ferrous metals (which are not produced in Belarus). The main role in such transactions belongs to the top management of enterprises (directors and their deputies) who have unprecedented freedom of action. Proceeds from export re-sales are not controlled by anyone outside the enterprise and are used at the discretion of top management, often for their personal use.

All enterprises depend on a particular central structure that combines administrative and political functions. Up to the summer of 1994 it was the Council of Ministers; now it is the President's administration. The main source of power of this structure is its ability to force the National Bank to issue cheap (often negative-interest) credit to selected enterprises. These credits have a two-fold function: first, they provide wages to employees of enterprises in financial trouble; second, they provide the top management with monetary resources necessary for transactions of the type described above.

The first function serves as an ultimate justification for cheap credit: people must receive their wages because the bad financial situation of the enterprise is not their fault. The National Bank is persuaded to issue cheap credit (which it sometimes has no hope of recovering) for the sake of political stability. The other side of the coin is that cheap credits provide top management with resources for transactions of questionable legality. This fact is a common knowledge but for obvious reasons accurate information about such activities is unavailable.

Thus, the existing power structures, vested interests and economic system are mutually reinforcing. Both workers and managers of large industrial enterprises live in the best of all worlds: they have the state's support without the state's control. They have no interest in changing the existing situation. This situation is perpetuated by decision-makers in the central government agencies. Privatization (especially of the kind that leaves enterprises in hands of employees and the government) will not change the situation, merely recognize the existing state of affairs. The continuation of soft budget constraints, which promote inefficiency and, combined with the lack of effective control, breeds illegal activities, is not caused by the existing system of formal property rights. More important factors are the political clout of large industrial enterprises (sometimes with hundreds of thousands of workers) and the phenomenon of monopoly in post-Soviet economies.

The problem of monopoly, so persistent in the centrally-planned economy, remains unsolved after mass privatization.[2] In many post-Soviet countries, for example, in Belarus and Russia, special government agencies have been established to tackle this problem. In Belarus, the task of reducing the undesirable consequences of the monopolist behavior of industrial enterprises is assigned to the Byelorussian State Committee for Anti-Monopoly Policy.

To eliminate monopoly completely is impossible, at least in the short run, because it is deeply rooted in the structure of the industrial system created in the Soviet period. A peculiar feature of the Soviet-style monopoly was the fact that not only large enterprises enjoyed monopolistic position. Virtually every enterprise, however small, was designed (both in organizational and technological sense) to be the sole supplier of a particular set of goods and services to a particular set of consumers. Since competition was deemed unnecessary and wasteful by Soviet economic thought, and this was reflected in economic policy, the number of enterprises producing the same (or a similar) commodity was kept to a minimum. Of course, employees of every enterprise try to retain its monopolistic position since it provides them with job and income security. This situation, where structural elements and the interests of workers and managers act to reinforce the existing monopoly, makes demonopolization of the Soviet-type economy a very difficult task indeed. As Andras Nagy put it: "It is easy to create monopolies but extremely difficult to break them up and to "create" competition. Even if they are broken up administratively, the firms previously comprising monopoly can still engage in collusion, which is difficult to stop." (Nagy, 1992, p. 305).

In the immediate post-Soviet period, just as in the time of the centrally planned Soviet economy, central authorities could not tackle the problem of monopoly at its root. Rather, they tried to deal with the consequences of monopoly by creating a redistributive mechanism which would prohibit enterprises from profiting from their monopolist positions. This task consists of two major elements: price control and income redistribution. Ironically, the same methods that had been crucial for the existence of the centrally planned economy were now intended to alleviate harmful consequences of one of its legacies.

In post-Soviet it was impossible to resort to all-embracing price controls, which did not work even in the late Soviet economy. Therefore, the authorities have to identify the scope of such control. This is done more or less arbitrarily. In Belarus, an enterprise is considered a monopoly if it controls over forty percent of market for a particular product.

Once an enterprise is identified as a monopoly, it is subject to price control and redistribution of the excessive income. The latter is deemed excessive if the profit margin exceeds 25 (in some cases 30) percent.[3] Everything above this limit is transferred to the state budget. These limits on the profit margins are difficult to calculate and monitor adequately. According to the Byelorussian accounting practice, the most detailed balance of the enterprise's financial operation is calculated and submitted to the state control agencies once a year.

The existing accounting practice does not adequately reflect the impact of inflation on all aspects of the enterprise's financial activities (Kovalyov, 1994, p. 130). In the existing conditions of hyperinflation it makes any assessment of income or profit margins of enterprises quite remote from the real state of affairs. Even if new accounting techniques are introduced that can account for distortions caused by hyperinflation, adequate monitoring of profit margins is still next to impossible. In the Soviet period enterprises learned how to avoid central price setting and price control in order to use their monopolistic positions. One of the most successful methods was to artificially increase production costs and thus decrease the profit margins they had to report to the controlling agencies. This method still works in the post-Soviet economy, effectively preventing the state control agencies from adequate assessment of the enterprise's financial situation.

Yet another way of reducing the monopolist behavior of enterprises in Belarus is so-called "declaration of prices". In fact, it is very similar to the central price setting in the Soviet-type economy. If an enterprise considered a monopoly raises the price of a particular product, it has to report the reasons for this rise to the State Committee for Price Control and to the Anti-Monopoly Committee. If these committees find that the rise was due to the factors outside the enterprise's control, they approve the new price. On the other hand, if it is found that the price increased solely due to the monopolist position of the enterprise, the rise is prohibited. In reality, however, this method works just as badly as the previous one and for the same reason. Enterprises have extensive experience in manipulating profit and cost figures as well as in negotiations with central authorities about new prices on their products. In today's chaotic economy it is particularly easy to persuade the controlling agencies that a price rise is due to increased cost caused in turn by increases in the prices of supplies.

Anti-monopoly measures in Belarus are not intended to eliminate monopoly. They do not attempt even to encourage cost reduction by monopolistic enterprises. The only thing they are designed to do is to make monopolistic behavior less profitable. As we have seen above, even this limited task applied to a limited number of monopolies is impossible to carry out. This is an indication that the existing monopoly of the Soviet type cannot be eradicated by measures similar to those that helped to create and maintain the over-monopolized economic system.

Monopoly can be effectively undermined only by increased competition. Direct state involvement in this process can only be quite modest. Increased competition can be achieved by opening of the economy to newly emerging companies as well as importing foreign goods and achieving significant new investments. The state can facilitate the former by eliminating non-economic obstacles for the newly emerging firms, abolishing protectionist import tariffs and encouraging foreign investments.[4] However, the crucial problem is to find a sufficient amount of capital to create new firms which would be competitive with the old monopolies. In this process the state cannot provide much help. Unfortunately, in the short run mass privatization cannot solve the problem of the lack of capital. Mass voucher privatization does not increase the volume of capital assets; it simply changes holders of property titles (in some cases even this is not completely accomplished). To raise the investments needed for restructuring is the task of the secondary market, where stocks are freely traded and their value fluctuates according to supply and demand. With a large supply of firms with obsolete equipment, low competitiveness, and recalcitrant workers, demand is bound to be low and so are share prices and subsequently investments. Potential investors would be interested in radical restructuring of enterprises which will inevitably entail reductions of the workforce, something that the workers almost certainly will not tolerate and which they can effectively oppose given their position as major collective stockholders.

Mass privatization is also influenced by processes in a particular social subsystem commonly known as civil society. In the context of post-Soviet transformations, the notion of civil society has become ideologized and value-laden. It implies something opposed to a Communist regime (which is true) and therefore taken to be inherently supportive of all aspects of post-Communist transitions. Moreover, in some countries civil society has become very much identified with particular political movements, such as Chapter 77 and later the Civic Forum in Czechoslovakia, Solidarity in Poland, and Sajudis in Lithuania, to the extent that they have been perceived as identical with civil society by some outside observers. All these movements included market reforms in their programs, albeit they did not envision the radical version of the market as a desirable state of the economy.

In Poland, civil society was thought to center around two social structures: Solidarity and the Roman Catholic Church. This led to a situation where these two alone were singled out by researchers as representatives of civil society, whereas the broader milieu of various social movements was to a large extent ignored (Cahalen, 1995). Since both Solidarity and the Roman Catholic Church strongly opposed the Communist regime, many political and economic reformers did not count them among opponents of market transition. However, neither of these two major groups accepted economic reforms and their implications in their entirety. On the other hand, there existed (and still exist) a multitude of other social movements, groups, and organizations -- not always interrelated, sometimes with loosely defined borders -- but clearly independent of the state and with their own agendas (Cahalen, 1995, p.199). For all practical purposes and in accordance with existing conceptual frameworks, these organizations can be regarded as constituent elements of civil society.[5] Even though some elements of economic reforms were generally welcomed by many major groups within civil society, "economically correct" privatization was not among them.

Janusz Lewandowski, one of the principal architects of Polish economic reforms and former Polish privatization minister once said that mass privatization is a device to "sell enterprises that nobody owns and nobody wants to people who cannot pay". Clearly, it was not this situation he and his colleagues hoped for when they were creating blueprints for economic reforms. However, extra-economic realities forced them to choose a less than economically optimal method of privatization.

It seems that enterprise that are inefficient and dependent on the state, although in some cases ostensibly privatized, will burden many post-Soviet transitional economies for many years. With the exception of Hungary, Estonia, and the Czech republic, where foreign investments into some of the existing privatized enterprises are more readily available, the restructuring process is likely to be protracted and conducted on a case by case basis rather than being swift and all-embracing.

It is very likely that mass privatization, initially regarded as the most promising path toward the market, will remain a long and gradual process with unexpected outcomes. The slow and inconsistent progress of mass privatization is not caused by lack of determination on the part of the government. As we have seen, the good intentions of the Polish reformers did not help them in their privatization efforts. For decades, the Soviet-type economy so closely intertwined economic and political subsystems of society that their immediate separation is in most cases simply impossible, regardless of the reformers' intentions.

However, the above negative arguments do not apply to the privatization of small-scale enterprises. In the former Soviet Union, and to some extent in Poland, even the small enterprises in services and retail trade had been owned and controlled by the state. In many post-Soviet countries, privatization of small economic units started earlier and has been much more successful than more ambitious plans to privatize large and medium-scale enterprises. This was the case in Poland and the Baltics, although much less so in Belarus.

Usually this process is conducted separately from the large-scale mass privatization programs. What makes the small-scale privatization different?

A small enterprise is easier to privatize than a large one. A small number of investors means that a clear-cut property title can be established, usually without a residual number of shares retained by the state. Even if the initial owners are the employees, their small number does not allow the separation of ownership and control, thus preventing the emergence of the "principal-agent" problem. Besides, unlike employees of a large enterprise, employees/owners of a small enterprise are less likely to rely upon profit reserves and asset-stripping for the immediate improvement of their living conditions. Profit reserves are likely to be small or non-existent; and asset-stripping -- given that small enterprises have very little slack -- will result in the disappearance of the enterprise. Therefore, owners of a small enterprise have to increase its efficiency in order to ensure its survival and their own well-being.

The most important difference between privatization of large and small enterprises is that the latter does not entail major political considerations. If large enterprises are politically important because of their sheer size and therefore in a position to demand continuing support from the state, small enterprises do not have the same political clout. The state can easily withdraw its direct support once these enterprises have been privatized.

Not only are the small enterprises easier to privatize (due to the absence of political constraints), but they also contribute to the development of a market economy to a larger extent than large enterprises. Because the "principal-agent" problem is non-existent for small enterprises, their incentives for efficient performance are not constrained by this controversy. Not surprisingly, most experienced and successful reformers list the development of the private sector through privatization of small assets among the top priorities of transitional policies (Balcerowicz and Gelb, 1994). In fact, privatization of the small enterprises can be regarded as the emergence of new small private firms via the acquisition of the previously state-owned assets by individual owners.

Performance levels of small-scale private enterprises cannot be measured in detail due to the lack of reliable data (the old statistical system tends to underestimate the performance of small private economic entities), but aggregate indicators suggest they are quite impressive. In Poland and Latvia, where by 1994 the large-scale privatization had not yet started and, consequently, most of large and medium enterprises still were controlled by the state, the private sector accounted for more than half of GNP in 1994. By 1995, the Polish private sector accounted for one third of industrial output, even though its fixed assets were only one sixth of the total (Poznanski, 1996, p. 280). In Lithuania, small private companies have higher efficiency and better overall performance than both remaining state-owned and the privatized large and medium firms (Semeta, 1995, p. 117). In Latvia, small private enterprises had absorbed a forty-four percent increase in the state sector unemployment between 1990 and 1993 (IMF, 1994b, p. 27). In transitional economies with stagnating enterprises still under government control and with successfully privatized firms undergoing painful restructuring (often with workforce reduction) small enterprises are becoming a major source of new jobs, thus alleviating rapid increase in unemployment.

Those countries where small enterprises were successfully privatized are making significant progress toward market economy. Whether this progress will lead to a modern capitalist economy similar to that of the developed capitalist countries, remains to be seen. However, its contribution to the emerging market is already well recognizable. In Poland, where small-scale privatization conducted by local governments had included more than 20,000 enterprises, private firms grew faster, hired a larger number of new employees, and invested more than state-owned enterprises (UN, 1996, p. 69). In all three Baltic states the situation was essentially the same. In Lithuania, Latvia, and Estonia privatization of small enterprises had been completed by 1994 and the private sector in all these countries accounted for 50 (Latvia) to 55 (Lithuania and Estonia) percent of GNP. At the same time, in Belarus, where privatization of small enterprises was much slower, the market is almost non-existent and the economy continues to decline (World Bank, 1997, p. xviii).

In Belarus, progress in small-scale privatization up to 1994 had been actually worse than that with the mass large-scale privatization (even though the latter had been bad enough). While in other countries of the region the privatized small enterprises (mostly in retail trade and services) were counted by the thousand, in Belarus they are still counted by single units. According to Belarus's Ministry of State Property and Privatization, in 1993 only two state-owned firms (one in retail trade and one in services) had been privatized by the small-scale privatization program. In the first half of 1994 this number was only six firms (one in retail trade, five in services). As of 1996, only 10 percent of small enterprises had been privatized (World Bank, 1997, p. xviii). In fact, even the modest progress of large-scale privatization in Belarus looks impressive if compared to the small-scale privatization.

As in many other post-Soviet countries, in Belarus small-scale privatization was conducted on the local level. This is a plausible approach since most enterprises in retail trade and services were controlled by local authorities. Their organizational structure needs to be briefly discussed to clarify the peculiarities of their privatization. Each enterprise in retail trade or services was not an independent unit but an integral part of a regional amalgamation under the management of the local authorities who in turn reported to the Ministry in Minsk. When privatization started, local authorities insisted that these regional amalgamations should be privatized as single units instead of being dissolved and each small unit privatized separately. Despite the efforts of the State Committee of Demonopolization and the Ministry of State Property and Privatization, local authorities succeeded in their attempts to establish the regional amalgamation as the unit subject to privatization. This explains the small number of privatized enterprises, since each of them consists sometimes of hundreds of small firms. Thus, small-scale privatization in Belarus had been essentially similar to large-scale privatization. Local authorities control supposedly privatized enterprises by retaining significant numbers of shares.

In Belarus, before all market reforms had been abandoned in 1994, the small-scale privatization program had made negligible progress. This seriously impeded the country's movement toward a market economy. Other countries of the region, with variable degrees of progress of large-scale privatization but universally successful small-scale privatization, had more than fifty percent of their GNP produced by the private sector. This seems to confirm that the emergence and development of small private enterprises can account for the relative success of market transition in Poland and the Baltic states and the lack of transition in Belarus, while the mass privatization is influenced by political considerations that often make it an economically artificial process.

In methodological terms, the above discussion suggests that when assessing progress of market reforms we should concentrate on the analysis of the emergence and development of small enterprises, the other two components being of more peripheral importance. However, we should remember that the emergence of small private enterprises, while indicating the development of a market economy, does not necessarily contribute to the emergence of a modern capitalist market. Small enterprises are inherently unstable and unable to bear large transaction costs, especially enforcement costs. They are vulnerable to non-economic methods of competition and cannot develop in a socially and politically unstable environment.

Market transition in Eastern Europe and the former Soviet Union is not driven mainly by deliberate government actions designed to change property rights by decree or through massive foreign investments, but rather by spontaneous individual actions of the multitude of small-scale entrepreneurs. This has some implications for the speed of transition to modern capitalist markets. The overall process of capital accumulation will be slow, due to a very small saving ratio in most transitional economies. Large-scale privatization processes, slow in speed and politically motivated, are unlikely to create conditions for restructuring and demonopolization of the privatized enterprises. Foreign investors are reluctant to provide the much needed capital unless elements of a market structure are already in place. The main factor in increasing economic efficiency is likely to be the growth and expansion of small private enterprises that will increase competition and force the large enterprises, often under joint control of employees and government agencies, to restructure or go bankrupt. But small enterprises will accumulate capital and expand only gradually, even if the state is able and willing to create and maintain the necessary conditions. The latter is by no means certain, given the ever-changing political climate in the post-Soviet world. The market reforms that began as a rapid movement toward a clearly defined goal, are turning into a slow process with uncertain outcome. For some time to come, private enterprises will co-exist with large government-controlled firms. Thus, even though the process of transformation is irreversible, its outcomes are likely to be more complex than those projected by the liberal interpretation of Property Rights theory.

The above discussion provides some insights into relations between power and property rights in transitional societies of post-Communist Eastern Europe. Patterns of political power distribution proved to differ significantly from the assumptions put forward by the activist interpretations of property rights theory. Instead of being concentrated at the top of social hierarchy, in the hands of high-ranking administrators and Party officials, power in the late Soviet and early post-Soviet societies was present at the level of industrial enterprise where it was shared by workers and management. Systemic transformation accompanied by the circulation of ruling elite does not entail immediate changes in the patterns of distribution of political power. It does facilitate the emergence of a new property rights system, but it does so by encouraging the development of new private firms rather than by rapidly transferring state-owned large enterprises into private hands. We can plausibly assume that in transitional societies political power and property rights are not closely connected but rather loosely related.

Notes

1   For the latest analysis of workers' behavior in the labor-managed Yugoslav enterprises and its consequences see: Pejovich, 1995, pp. 152-53 and 209-27.

2   This problem is rooted in the main principles of the Soviet-type economy. Monopolies were created deliberately in the course of industrialization in the Soviet Union and its satellite states. They provided economies of scale within the centrally established division of labor and could be controlled by the central economic authorities.

3   For some enterprises, for example in the food processing industry, this limit is set at 5 percent.

4   Foreign direct investments do not always reduce the number of monopolies. As Nagy points out, investment into the existing monopolies is often considered more profitable than establishing new competing firms (Nagy, 1992, p. 305).

5   For example, Weigle and Butterfield define civil society as "the independent self-organization of society, the constituent parts of which voluntarily engage in public activity to pursue individual, group, or national interests within the legally defined state-society relationship" (1992, p. 3).

Conclusion

Post-Communist societies of Eastern Europe and the former Soviet Union display a complex, contradictory, and uneven pattern of socio-economic transformations. Interestingly enough, the economic component of this process is all too often explained in simplified terms, equating transformation (a not necessarily controllable and predictable process of change) with transition from some known point of departure to an equally well known outcome. Further reducing the complex reality of transformation process, transition is often equated with reforms, i.e. deliberate, conscious, and concerted actions. This reductionist approach is exhibited by proponents of neo-liberal economics, who without hesitation apply its theoretical apparatus not only to the model of economic system to be created by post-Communist market reforms, but also to the process of transformation itself. Their reasoning is based on the following assumptions: experts possess perfect knowledge of the desirable economic system as well as the procedures of transition; politicians, driven by considerations of economic efficiency, are willing and able to conduct market reforms according to experts' advice.

In my book I question these assumptions and examine the real state of knowledge about market economy in the late Communist societies as well as the motives of the opposition politicians who, after they came to power, started market reforms. The research is based on a comparative analysis of five post-Communist countries: Poland, Belarus, Lithuania, Latvia, and Estonia. Despite very similar economic systems prior to the collapse of Soviet domination these countries are exhibiting significant cross-national variations in their post-Soviet developments. This is particularly true for Belarus compared to the rest of the countries in my study. In the years that passed since the completion of this research these trends became even more divergent. Poland's GDP surpassed its pre-reform level and continues to grow steadily despite the continuing strength of political forces with Communist past. In the three Baltic states economies remain vibrant and rapidly modernizing. At the same time, in all these countries large industrial enterprises inherited from the Soviet-type economy remain a burdensome responsibility of state agencies and their privatization does not seem to be rapidly progressing. On the other hand, Belarus's adherence to the Soviet-type economic system, supported by barter trade with Russia, is even more pronounced. Thus, the recent developments do not contradict main ideas of this book.

There is no specific theory of socio-economic development that could predict or explain post-Communist transformations in Eastern Europe and the former Soviet Union. As we have seen in Chapter One, theories that purport to explain socio-economic changes in particular countries as part of a global process do not provide a plausible explanation of cross-national variations in our case. This is particularly true of World System Theory which focuses on the external economic factors to explain changes in individual countries. The interpretations of Modernization Theory that assign the primary significance to the universal processes of differentiation and adaptation are too general to provide sufficiently detailed explanations of post-Communist developments.

The most ambitious and activist approach to the transition from the state-controlled to the market economy is based on the neo-liberal economic model. For several years it has been widely used not only as an analytical tool, but also as a foundation for reform policies in post-Communist countries. Its influence is enhanced by the fact that, as many observers (e.g. Lavigne, 1995; Slay, 1995) note, it represents the only detailed concept of transition. However, the use of neo-liberal frame of reference for the analysis of post-Communist transformations resulted in the loss of its internal logical consistency. In the original neo-classical economic paradigm, based on the Utilitarian-Positivist tradition, the main actor is a rational, well-informed individual who acts to maximize his/her material benefits. In the version of this paradigm applied to post-Communist economic transformations this premiss has undergone a strange modification. Now, the main agent of economic reforms is a rational, well-informed *government* that acts to maximize efficiency of the economy as a whole. Ironically, this image resembles an idealized picture of Soviet economic bureaucracy, which even in its heyday was neither efficient nor well-informed. When their vision of market progress fails to materialize, neo-liberal reformers resort to a circular argument, insisting that the reality differs from their projections because their assumptions have not been met. In so doing, they, perhaps unwittingly, admit that there is more to post-Communist economic transformations than the rational and deliberate pursuit of economic efficiency.

In fact, as we have seen in Chapter Two, Communist leaders in the years prior to the collapse of the Soviet system were much more concerned with improvements in economic efficiency than were the emerging opposition politicians. Leaders of the major opposition movements did not count higher economic performance among their primary goals. They were much more concerned with the social aspects of alternative economic arrangements. Whatever elements of the market they were prepared to include into their projected economic models, the sum of these elements never amounted to the laissez-faire market economy. Indeed, attitude of the opposition leaders toward the market was quite cautious.

Knowledge about the modern capitalist market economy among the experts of the late Soviet period was far from perfect. In fact, most economists possessed little adequate knowledge of the market while their understanding of market transition was even more limited. The official economic discourse was dominated by the problems of restructuring of the Soviet-type economy and enhancing its efficiency. In the Baltics, the nationally-minded economists were able to use this discourse to assert their republics' rights to control their resources. At the same time, there started to emerge a dialogue between the opposition politicians and the economists. This dialogue, however, did not result in the adoption of the free-market economic model by the nationalist opposition, largely due to the fact that neither the opposition leaders nor their economic experts were sufficiently familiar with the market paradigm. In addition to that, the opposition intellectuals were suspicious of the free market which they saw as a potential threat to national community and civil society they intended to create.

In their vision of economic reforms, neo-liberal economists tacitly assume that the existing Soviet-type bureaucracy will cooperate with the reformist politicians and experts. However, as we have seen in Chapter Three, bureaucrats are not neutral. Instead, they have their own agendas that often are influenced by the existing value-patterns. The legitimation of economic policies is based on the values and orientations of non-economic nature. In the Baltics the market reforms were legitimized in nationalist terms. This, among other things, allowed to successfully exclude the Russian-speaking opponents of reforms from participating in discussion of technical aspects of reform policies. In Poland, the market reforms were legitimized in terms of national revival, breaking with the Russian-dominated Soviet system, and return to the "normal" European path of development. In both cases, the legitimation of reforms in terms of the prevailing national values and orientations helped to implement crucial elements of trade liberalization (in the Baltics) and macro-economic stabilization (in Poland). On the other hand, in Belarus, where politicians, bureaucrats, and the general public all possessed rather weak national consciousness and where positive orientations toward Russia were especially prevalent among bureaucrats, the ruling elite maintained the old

Soviet-type economic arrangements as long as they helped to preserve the ties with Russia.

Thus, the reality of post-Communist economic transformations is markedly different from assumptions of neo-liberal reformers. In fact, politicians do not initiate market reforms on the basis of rational calculation. Economic experts are not sufficiently well-informed. Bureaucrats are not neutral. The post-Soviet transformations can be regarded as unintended consequences of the actions directly unrelated to market reforms. They were brought about by the new elites who were often suspicious of market, did not know how it works, and seldom had economic efficiency on the list of their top priorities. When the nationalist leaders in the Baltics started their quest for national independence, they did not realize that it will entail attempts of radical market reforms. In Poland, some elements of market reform (monetary stabilization and economic liberalization) had been of instrumental significance while others (e.g. mass privatization) had been of rather symbolic nature.

Even in successful cases, market transition is not an essentially one-step process of shifting from one economic model with low performance to another, almost equally well known model with superior performance. Instead, it is a spontaneously emerging chain of relatively isolated steps, each with its own vector of preferences (not exclusively of economic nature) and system of constraints (mostly of non-economic nature).

Bibliography

Alchian, A. (1950), 'Uncertainty, Evolution and Economic Theory', *Journal of Political Economy*, Vol. 58, no.3, pp. 211-221.

Alexander, J. (1983), *The Modern Reconstruction of Classical Thought: Talcott Parsons*, University of California Press, Berkeley.

Antsipenka, A. (1992), 'Natsiyanal'naya Elita: Typy yak Antytypy' ('National Elite: the Types and the Anti-Types'), *Litaratura i Mastatstva*, 14 August 1992.

Aron, R. (1965), *Main Currents of Sociological Thought*, Doubleday, New York.

Aslund, A. (1992), *Post-Communist Economic Revolutions: How Big A Bang?*, The Center for Strategic and International Studies, Washington, DC.

Aujac, H. (1984), 'Cultures and Growth', in M. Seligson (ed.), *The Gap Between Rich and Poor*, Westview Press, Boulder, CO, pp. 38-52.

Balcerovicz, L. and Gelb, A. (1994), 'How to Stabilize -- Policy Lessons From Early Reformers' *Transition*, Vol.5 (May - June), p. 4.

Beissinger, M. (1996), 'How Nationalisms Spread: Eastern Europe Adrift the Tides and Cycles of Nationalist Contention', *Social Research*, Vol. 63, no.1, pp. 97-145.

Bernhard, M. (1993), *The Origins of Democratization in Poland: Workers, Intellectuals, and Oppositional Politics, 1976-1980*, Columbia University Press, New York.

Bottomore, T. (1991), *Classes in Modern Society*, Harper Collins, London.

Bottomore, T. (1993), *Elites and Society*, Routledge, New York.

Boycko, M., Shleifer, A. and Vishny, R.W. (1995), 'Mass privatization in Russia', in *Mass Privatization: An Initial Assessment*, Organization for Economic Cooperation and Development, Paris, pp. 153-190.

Brada, J. (1992), 'Political Economy of East European-Soviet Trade: Rethinking the Past and Searching for the Future', in K. Poznanski (ed.), *Constructing Capitalism: The Reemergence of Civil Society and Liberal Economy in the Post-Communist World*, Westview Press, Boulder, CO, pp. 47-70.

Bronshtein, M. (1993), 'Comment', in J. Williamson (ed.), *Economic Consequences of Soviet Disintegration*, Institute for International Economics, Washington, D.C., pp. 513-518.

Bunce, V. (1992), 'Two-Tiered Stalinism: A Case of Self-Destruction', in K. Poznanski (ed.), *Constructing Capitalism: The Reemergence of Civil Society and Liberal Economy in the Post-Communist World*, Westview Press, Boulder, CO, pp. 25-46.

Burszta, W. (1995), 'Return of the Magi', *Polish Sociological Review*, Vol. 3 (107), pp. 212-217.

Byelorussian Academy of Sciences (1988), *O Perekhode BSSR k Usloviyam Territorial'nogo Samofinansirovaniya, (On Transition of BSSR to Conditions of Territorial Self-financing)* Byelorussian Academy of Sciences, Minsk.

Byelorussian State Committee for Anti-Monopoly Policy (1994), *Kompleksnaya Programma Demonopolizatsii Narodnogo Khoziaistva Respubliki Belarus (A Complex Program of Demonopolization of the National Economy of the Republic of Belarus)*, prepared by the Byelorussian State Committee for Anti-Monopoly Policy, Minsk.

Byelorussian State Planning Committee (1988) *O Perekhode BSSR k Usloviyam Territorial'nogo Samofinansirovaniya, (On Transition of BSSR to Conditions of Territorial Self-financing)*, Byelorussian State Planning Committee, Minsk.

Cahalen, D. (1995), 'A Place to Stand: Social Movements and Civil Society in Poland', *Polish Sociological Review*, Vol 3 (107), pp. 200-210.

Chekmonas, V. (1989), 'Polonizatsiya Pol'skogo Etnosa na Vilenschizne' ('Polonization of the Polish Ethnic Group in the Vilnius Region'), *Soglasie*, 22 May.

Chirot, D.(1977), *Social Change in the Twentieth Century*, Harcourt, Brace, Jovanovich, New York.

Coase, R. (1988), *The Firm, the Market, and the Law*, The University of Chicago Press, Chicago.

Cooter, R. (1991), 'Organizational Property and Privatization in Russia', in B. L. Smith and G. M. Danilenko (eds), *Law and Democracy in the New Russia*, The Brookings Institution, Washington, D.C., pp. 53-71.

Csaba, L. (1995), *The Capitalist Revolution in Eastern Europe*, Edward Elgar Publishing Company, Aldershot.

Dallin, A. (1957), *German Rule in Russia*, Macmillan, London.

Earle, J., Frydman, R., Rapaczinski, A. and Turkewitz, J. (1994), *Small Privatization: The Transformation of Retail Trade and Consumer Services in The Czech Republic, Hungary, and Poland*, Central European University Press, Budapest.

Easterly, W. and Fisher, S. (1994), *The Soviet Economic Decline: Historical and Republican Data*, World Bank Working Paper, no. 1284, World Bank, Washington, D.C.

'Economic Program of Sajudis' (1990), *Voprosy Ekonomiki*, no.3, pp. 88-89.

'Economic Program of the Estonian Popular Front' (1990), *Voprosy Ekonomiki*, no.3, pp. 89-91.

Eisenstadt, S. (1963), *The Political System of Empires*, Free Press, New York.

European Bank for Reconstruction and Development (EBRD) (1994), *Report on Economic Transition in Eastern Europe and the Former Soviet Union in 1994*, European Bank for Reconstruction and Development, London.

European Bank for Reconstruction and Development (EBRD) 1997, *Transition Report 1997*, European Bank for Reconstruction and Development, London.

Evans, P. (1989), 'Predatory, Developmental, and Other Apparatuses: A Comparative Political Economy Perspective on the Third World State', *Sociological Forum*, Vol. 4 (December), pp. 561-587.

George, K. (1991), 'Public Ownership versus Privatization', in *Competition in Europe: Essays in Honor of Henk de Jong*, P. de Wolf (ed.), Kluwer Academic Publishers, Dordrecht pp. 163-186.

Goodwin, L. (1991), *Breaking The Barrier: The Rise of Solidarity in Poland*, Oxford University Press, New York.

Gross, J. (1988), *Revolution from Abroad. The Soviet Conquest of Poland's Western Ukraine and Western Byelorussia*, Princeton University Press, Princeton, N.J.

Habermas, J. (1975), *Legitimation Crisis*, Beacon Press, Boston.

Habermas, J. (1990), 'What Does Socialism Mean Today? The Rectifying Revolution and the Need for New Thinking on the Left', *New Left Review*, No. 183, (September-October), pp. 3-22.

Hermann-Pillath, C. (1993), 'Informal Constraints, Culture, and Incremental Transition from Plan to Market', in H.-J. Wagener (ed.), *On The Theory and Policy of Systemic Change*, Physica-Verlag, Heidelberg, pp. 95-120.

Holzman, F. (1962), 'Soviet Foreign Trade Pricing and the Question of Discrimination', *Review of Economics and Statistics*, Vol. 44, no.2 (May), pp. 134-147.

Holzman, F. (1965), 'More on Soviet Bloc Trade Discrimination', *Soviet Studies*, Vol. 17, no.1 (July), pp. 44-65.

Holzman, F. (1976), *International Trade Under Communism*, Basic Books, New York.

Hopkins, T. (1982), 'World-System Analysis: Methodological Issues', in T. Hopkins and I. Wallerstein (eds), *World-System Analysis: Theory and Methodology*, Sage Publications, London, pp. 145-158.

Huntington, S. (1968), *Political Order in Changing Societies*, Yale University Press, New Haven, CT.

Ickes, B. and Ryterman, R. (1992), 'The Interenterprise Arrears Crisis in Russia', *Post-Soviet Affairs*, Vol. 8, no.4, pp. 331-361.

International Monetary Fund (IMF) (1994a), *Economic Review: Belarus*, International Monetary Fund, Washington, D.C.

International Monetary Fund (IMF) (1994b), *Economic Review: Estonia*, International Monetary Fund, Washington, D.C.

International Monetary Fund (IMF) (1994c), *Economic Review: Latvia*, International Monetary Fund, Washington, D.C.

International Monetary Fund (IMF) (1994d), *Economic Review: Lithuania*, International Monetary Fund, Washington, D.C.

Ivanov, M. (1991), 'The Byelorussians of Eastern Poland under Soviet Occupation, 1939-1941', in K. Sword (ed.), *The Soviet Takeover of the Polish Eastern Provinces, 1939-41*, St. Martin's Press, New York, pp. 253-254.

Johnson, C. (1982), *Revolutionary Change*, Stanford University Press, Stanford, CA.

Karklins, R. (1994), *Ethnopolitics and Transition to Democracy: The Collapse of The USSR and Latvia*, Woodrow Wilson Center Press, Washington, D.C.

Kebich, W. (1993), 'Nash Piotr Mironovich' ('Our Piotr Mironovich'), *Zviazda*, April 10.

Kebich, W. (1994) 'Interview', *Belaya Rus'*, May 20.

Keerna, A. (1988), 'Khozraschiot Regional'nyi' ('Regional Self-financing'), *Voprosy Ekonomiki*, no.8, pp. 65-76.

Kehris, O. (1989), 'Ob Ekonomicheskoi Modeli Latvii' ('On Latvian Economic Model'), *Atmoda*, 27 March.

Kennedy, M. (1991), *Professionals, Power, and Solidarity in Poland*, Cambridge University Press, London.

Keynes, J. M. (1923 [1963]), 'Social Consequences of Changes in the Value of Money', in J. M. Keynes, *Essays in Persuasion*, W.W. Norton & Co, New York, pp. 80-104.

Keynes, J. M. (1925 [1963]), 'A Short View of Russia' in J. M. Keynes, *Essays in Persuasion*, W.W. Norton & Co, New York, pp. 297-311.

Keynes, J. M. (1936 [1964]), *The General Theory of Employment, Interest, and Money*, Harcourt, Brace & World, New York.

Khanin, G. (1988), 'Ekonomicheskii Rost: Alternativnaya Otsenka' ('Economic Growth: an Alternative Assessment'), *Kommunist*, no. 17, pp.83-90.

Koeves, A. (1983), 'Implicit Subsidies and Some Issues of Economic Relations within CMEA', *Acta Oeconomica*, Vol. 31, no.1-2, pp. 125-136.

Kolakovski, L. (1992), 'Mind and Body: Ideology and Economy in the Collapse of Communism', in K. Poznanski (ed.), *Constructing Capitalism: the Reemergence of Civil Society and Liberal Economy in the Post-Communist World*, Westview Press, Boulder, CO, pp. 9-24.

Kolganov, A. and Buzgalin, A. (1988), 'Kak Byla Vozdvignuta Administrativnaya Sistema' ('How the Administrative System Had Been Built'), *Voprosy Ekonomiki*, no. 12, pp. 25-34.

Konrad, G. and Szelenyi, I. (1979), *The Intellectuals on the Road to Class Power*, Harvester, Boston.

Kornai, J. (1990), *The Road to a Free Economy. Shifting from a Socialist System: The Example of Hungary*, W.W. Norton and Company, New York.

Kornai, J. (1992), *The Socialist System: the Political Economy of Communism*, Princeton University Press, Princeton, N.J.

Kovalyov, L., Mikhailova-Staniuta, I and Shuleiko, O. (1994), *Otsenka Finansovogo Sostoyaniya Predpriyatiya (Evaluation of Financial Situation of an Enterprise)*, Navuka i Tekhnika, Minsk.

Kulig, J. and Lipowski, A. (1994), *"Shock Therapy" in Poland: The Response of State-Owned Enterprises*, International Center for Economic Growth, San Francisco.

Laitin, D. (1995), 'National Revivals and Violence', *Archives Europeennes de Sociologie*, Vol. XXXVI, no. 1, pp. 3-43.

Lavigne, M. (1995), *The Economics of Transition*, St. Martin's Press, New York.

Levitas, A. (1994), 'Rethinking Reform: Lessons from Polish Privatization', in V. Milor, (ed.), *Changing Political Economies: Privatization in Post-Communist and Reforming Communist States*, Lynn Rienner Publishers, London, pp. 99-113.

Lichtheim, G. (1961), *Marxism*, London: Routledge and Kegan Paul.

Lieberman, I. (1995), 'Mass Privatization in Central and Eastern Europe and the Former Soviet Union: A Comparative Analysis', in *Mass Privatization: An Initial Assessment*, Organization for Economic Cooperation and Development, Paris, pp. 13-38.

Liepa, L. (1989), 'Radikal'nyi, Real'nyi, Eksperimental'nyi' ('Radical, Realistic, Experimental'), *Atmoda*, 10 June.

Lieven, A. (1993), *The Baltic Revolution*, Yale University Press, New Haven, CT.

Lijphart A. (1971), 'Comparative Politics and Comparative Method', *American Political Science Review*, Vol. 65, no. 3.

Lipski, J. (1985), *KOR: A History of Workers' Defense Committee in Poland, 1976-1981*, University of California Press, Berkeley.

Lubachko, I. (1972), *Byelorussia under Soviet Rule, 1917-1957*, The University Press of Kentucky, Lexington, KY.

Lych, G. and Nikitenko, M. (1991), 'Ekonomicheskaya Samostoyatel'nost' Respubliki v Usloviyakh Prekhoda k Rynochnoy Ekonomike' ('Economic Autonomy of the Republic in Conditions of Transition to the Market Economy'), *Voprosy Ekonomiki*, no.3, pp. 128-144.

Marrese, M. and Vanous, J. (1983), *Soviet Subsidization of Trade with Eastern Europe: A Soviet Perspective*, University of California Press, Berkeley.

Medvedev, P. and Nit, I. (1988), 'Nominal'niye Tseli i Real'naya Effektivnost' Ekonomicheskogo Upravleniya' ('Nominal Goals and Real Efficiency of Economic Management'), *Voprosy Ekonomiki*, no.12, pp. 46-54.

Menderhausen, H. (1959), 'Terms of Trade Between the Soviet Union and Smaller Communist Countries', *Review of Economics and Statistics*, Vol. 41, no.2 (May), pp. 106-118.

Menderhausen, H. (1960), 'The Terms of Soviet Satellite Trade', *Review of Economics and Statistics*, Vol. 42, no. 2 (May), pp. 152-163.

Milor, V. (1994), 'Changing Political Economies: an Introduction', in *Changing Political Economies: Privatization in Post-Communist and Reforming Communist States,* V. Milor (ed.), Lynn Rienner Publishers, London, pp. 1-26.

Motyl, A. (1990), *Sovietology, Rationality, Nationality*. Columbia University Press, New York.

Mouzelis, N. (1993), 'Evolution and Democracy: Talcott Parsons and the Collapse of Eastern European Regimes', *Theory, Culture and Society*, Vol. 10, pp.145-151.

Mueller, K. (1992), 'Modernizing Eastern Europe: Theoretical Problems and Dilemmas', *European Sociological Archive*, Vol. 33, pp.109-149.

Murrell, P. (1992), 'Evolution in Economics and the Economic Reform of the Centrally Planned Economies', in C. Clague and G. C. Rausser (eds), *The Emergence of Market Economies in Eastern Europe,* Blackwell, New York, pp. 35-54.

Nagy, A. (1992), 'Institutions and the Transition to a Market Economy', in C. Clague and G. Rausser (eds), *The Emergence of Market Economies in Eastern Europe,* Blackwell, Cambridge, MA.

Nahaylo, B. and Swoboda, V.(1990), *Soviet Disunion,* The Free Press, New York.

Nellis, J. (1994), 'Successful Privatization in Estonia: unusual Features', *Transition,* Vol. 5, (July-August), p. 5.

Newbery, D. (1992), 'The Safety Net During Transformation: Hungary', in C. Clague and G. C. Rausser (eds), *The Emergence of Market Economies in Eastern Europe,* Blackwell, New York, pp. 197-218.

Nordhaus, W. (1991), 'Stabilizing the Soviet Economy', in M. J. Peck and T. J. Richardson, (eds), *What Is To Be Done? Proposals for the Soviet Transition to the Market,* Yale University Press, New Haven, CT, pp. 83-115.

North, D. (1971), 'Institutional Change and Economic Growth', *Journal of Economic History,* Vol. 31.

North, D. (1981), *Structure and Change in Economic History,* Norton, New York.

North, D. (1990), *Institutions, Institutional Change and Economic Performance,* Cambridge University Press, Cambridge.

Novikova, L, Ovsiannikov, A. and Rotman, D. (1989), 'Stereotipy Istoricheskogo Samosoznaniya' ('Stereotypes of Historical Self-Consciousness'), *Sotsiologicheskiye Issledovaniya,* no. 5, pp. 3-12.

Olson, M. (1982), *The Rise and Decline of Nations: Economic Growth, Stagflation, and Social Rigidities,* Yale University Press, New Haven, CT.

Olson, M. (1993), 'The Hidden Path to a Successful Economy', in C. Clague and G. Rausser (eds), *The Emergence of Market Economies in Eastern Europe,* Blackwell, Cambridge, MA, pp. 55-76.

Pajestka, J. (1987), *Analiza Processów Reformowania Gospodarki (Analysis of the Processes of Economic Reforms),* Ossolineum, Warsaw.

Parsons, T. (1937 [1968]), *The Structure of Social Action,* The Free Press, New York.

Parsons, T. (1951), *The Social System,* The Free Press, New York.

Parsons, T. and Smelser, A. (1956), *Economy and Society,* The Free Press, New York.

Parsons, T. (1960), 'Authority, Legitimation, and Political Action', in T. Parsons, *Structure and Process in Modern Societies,* The Free Press, New York, pp. 199-225.

Parsons, T. (1964), 'Communism and the West: the Sociology of the Conflict', in A. Etzioni and E. Etzioni (eds), *Social Change: Sources, Patterns, and Consequences,* Basic Books, New York.

Parsons, T. (1969), *Politics and Social Structure,* The Free Press, New York.

Parsons, T. (1977), 'Comparative Studies and Evolutionary Change', in T. Parsons, *Social Systems and Evolution of Action Theory*, The Free Press, New York, pp. 279-320.

Patinkin, D. (1989), *Money, Interest, and Prices*, MIT Press, Cambridge, MA.

Pejovich, S. (1969), 'The Firm, Monetary Policy and Property Rights', *Western Economic Journal*, Vol. 7.

Pejovich, S. (1995), *Economic Analysis of Institutions and Systems*, Kluwer Academic Publishers, Dordrecht.

Pelikan, P. (1993), 'The Dynamics of Economic System', in H.-J. Wagener (ed.), *On The Theory and Policy of Systemic Change*, Physica-Verlag, Heidelberg, pp. 67-94.

Pickel, A. (1996), 'Official Ideology? The Role of Neoliberal Economic Reform Doctrines in Post-Communist Transformation', *Polish Sociological Review*, Vol. 4 (112), pp. 361-376.

Pletniov, E. (1988), 'Vozrastaniye Znacheniya Politicheskoy Ekonomii v Usloviyakh Perekhoda k Novomu Kachestvu Ekonomicheskogo Rosta' ('Increased Significance of Political Economy in Conditions of the Transition to the Qualitatively New Economic Growth'), *Voprosy Ekonomiki*, no.12, pp. 136-144.

Polanyi, K.(1944 [1957]), *The Great Transformation*, Beacon Press, Boston.

'Polish Privatization Fund Starts Trading with a Bang' *Wall Street Journal*, June 13, 1997

Popov, G. (1988), 'Zhurnal -- Perestroike' ('The Journal's Contribution to Perestroika'), *Voprosy Ekonomiki*, no.7, pp. 3-10.

Portes, A. (1994), 'The Informal Economy and its Paradoxes', in N. Smelser and R. Swedberg (eds), *The Handbook of Economic Sociology*, Princeton University Press, Princeton, N.J., pp. 426-451.

Poznanski, K. (1992), 'Property Rights Perspective on Evolution of Communist-Type Economies', in K. Poznanski (ed.), *Constructing Capitalism: the Reemergence of Civil Society and Liberal Economy in the Post-Communist World*, Westview Press, Boulder, CO, pp. 71-96.

'Program of the Belarusian Popular Front' (1990), Voprosy Ekonomiki, no.5, pp. 117-121.

Prunskene, K. (1989), 'Ob Ekonomicheskoy Samostoyatel'nosti Pribaltiyskikh Respublik' ('On Economic Independence of the Baltic Republics'), *Voprosy Ekonomiki*, no.12, pp.3-10.

Rigby, T.H. (1990), *Political Elites in the USSR*, Edward Elgar Publishing Company, Aldershot.

Rueschemeyer, D. (1986), *Power and the Division of Labour*, Stanford University Press, Stanford, CA.

Rueschemeyer, D. and Skocpol, T. (1996), 'Conclusion', in D. Rueschemeyer and T. Skocpol (eds), *States, Social Knowledge, and the Origins of Modern Social Policies*, Princeton University Press, Princeton, N.J. pp. 296-312.

Sachs, J. and Lipton, D. (1991), 'Shock Therapy and Real Incomes', *Financial Times*, 29 January.

Sachs, J. (1994), 'Life in the Economic Emergency Room', in J. Williamson (ed.), *The Political Economy of Policy Reform*, Institute for International Economics, Washington, D.C., pp. 501-523.

Sadowski, Z. (1987), *Zarządanie Gospodarką (Macroeconomic Management)*, Ossolineum, Warsaw.

Semeta, A. (1995), 'Post-Privatization Secondary Markets in Lithuania', in *Mass Privatization: An Initial Assessment*, Organization for Economic Cooperation and Development, Paris, pp. 121-134.

Shen, R. (1994), *Restructuring The Baltic Economies*, Praeger, Westport, CT.

Simenas, A. (1995), 'Privatization in Lithuania' in *Mass Privatization: An Initial Assessment*, Organization for Economic Cooperation and Development, Paris, pp. 107-120.

Skocpol, T.and Somers, M. (1980), 'The Uses of Comparative History in Macrosocial Inquiry', *Comparative Studies in Society and History*, Vol. 22, no. 2, pp. 174-197.

Skocpol, T. (1979), *States and Social Revolutions*, Cambridge University Press, Cambridge.

Slay, B. (1994), *The Polish Economy*, Princeton University Press, Princeton, N.J.

Smelser, N. (1994), *Sociology*, Blackwell, Oxford.

Smith, T. (1984), 'Reiterating the Identity of the Peripheral state', in M. Seligson (ed.), *The Gap Between Rich and Poor*, Westview Press, Boulder, CO, pp. 133-150.

Staniszkis, J. (1992), 'Main Paradoxes of the Democratic Change in Eastern Europe', in K. Poznanski (ed.), *Constructing Capitalism: the Reemergence of Civil Society and Liberal Economy in the Post-Communist World*, Westview Press, Boulder, CO, pp. 179-198.

Stark, D. (1994), 'Path Dependence and Privatization Strategies in East-Central Europe', in V.Milor (ed.), *Changing Political Economies: Privatization in Post-Communist and Reforming Communist States*, Lynn Rienner Publishers, London, pp. 115-145.

Steinbuka, I. (1993), 'The Baltics', in J. Williamson (ed.), *Economic Consequences of Soviet Disintegration*, Institute for International Economics, Washington, D.C., pp. 482-509.

Stinchcombe, A. (1968), *Constructing Social Theories*, The University of Chicago Press, Chicago.

Suleja, W. (1994), 'Mit Solidarnosci' ('The Myth of Solidarity'), in W. Wrzesinski (ed.), *Polskie Mity Polityczne XIX i XX Wieku (Polish Political Myths of the 19th and 20th Centuries)*, Wydawnictwo Uniwersytetu Wrocławskiego, Wroclaw, pp. 227-242.

Sutela, P. (1991), *Economic Thought and Economic Reform in the Soviet Union*, Cambridge University Press, Cambridge.

Swedberg, R. (1994) 'Markets as Social Structures', N. Smelser and R. Swedberg (eds), *The Handbook of Economic Sociology*, Princeton University Press, Princeton, N.J., pp. 255-282.

Swiatkowski, L. (1994), 'Quotation of the Month: "Privatization in Poland Will Remain a Political Battleground "', *Transition*, Vol. 5 (September), p. 2.

Tausch, A. (1993), *Towards a Socio-Liberal Theory of World Development*, St. Martin's Press, New York.

Thieme, J. (1995), 'The Polish Mass Privatization Program', in *Mass Privatization: An Initial Assessment*, Organization for Economic Cooperation and Development, Paris, pp. 39-46.

Tsvikevich, A. (1927), 'Ab Saramlivykh Dapushchen'niakh' ('About Shameful Admissions'), *Polymia*, Vol. 3, pp. 23-38.

Turner, J. and Beeghley, L. (1982), *The Emergence of Sociological Theory*, The Dorsey Press, Homewood, IL.

UN (1996), *Economic Survey of Europe in 1995-1996*, United Nations, Geneva.

Uno, K. (1991), 'Privatization and the Creation of a Commercial Banking System', in M. J. Peck and T. J. Richardson (eds), *What Is To Be Done? Proposals for the Soviet Transition to the Market*, Yale University Press, New Haven, CT, pp. 149-178.

Urban, M. (1989), *An Algebra of Soviet Power: Elite Circulation in the Byelorussian Republic, 1966-86*, Cambridge University Press, Cambridge.

Vakar, N. (1956), *Belorussia. The Making of a Nation*, Harvard University Press, Cambridge, MA.

Vasil'ev, V. (1989), 'Khoziaistvennyi Mekhanizm Soyuznoy Respubliki' ('Economic System of a Constituent Republic'), *Voprosy Ekonomiki*, no.12, pp. 11-19.

Wagener, H.-J. (1993), 'Some Theory of Systemic Change and Transformation', in H.-J. Wagener (ed.), *On The Theory and Policy of Systemic Change*, Physica-Verlag, Heidelberg, pp. 1-20.

Wallerstein, I. (1984), 'The Present State of the Debate on World Inequality', in M. Seligson (ed.), *The Gap Between Rich and Poor*, Westview Press, Boulder, CO, pp. 119-132.

Wallerstein, I. (1984a), *The Politics of the World-Economy*, Cambridge University Press, Cambridge.

Walton, J. (1992), *Western Times and Water Wars: State, Culture and Rebellion in California*, University of California Press, Berkeley.

Weigle, M. A. and Butterfield, J. (1992), 'Civil Society in Reforming Communist Regimes: the Logic of Emergence', *Comparative Politics*, Vol.25, no.1, pp.1-23.

Welfens, P. (1992), *Market-Oriented Systemic Transformation in Eastern Europe*, Springer Verlag, Heidelberg.

Williamson, J. (1993), 'Trade and Payments after Soviet Disintegration', in J. Williamson (ed.), *Economic Consequences of Soviet Disintegration*, Institute for International Economics, Washington, D.C., pp. 558-632.

Winiecki, J. (1990), *Resistance to Change in the Soviet Economic System*, Routledge, New York.

Winiecki, J. (1995), 'Polish Mass Privatization Program: The Unloved Child in a Suspect Family', in *Mass Privatization: An Initial Assessment*, Organization for Economic Cooperation and Development, Paris, pp. 47-60.

World Bank, (1997), *Belarus: Prices, Markets, and Enterprise Reform*, The World Bank, Washington, D.C.

Zalamai, I. (1993), 'Interview', *Zviazda*, September 7.

Żidovicz, K. (1994), 'Fatalne Uzależnie -- Mieć Albo Nie Mieć' ('Fatal Dependency: To Have or Not To Have'), *Eurazja*, no. 3-4, pp.40-47.

Zuzovski, R. (1992), *Political Dissent and Opposition in Poland*, Praeger, Westport, CT.

Index

For Product Safety Concerns and Information please contact our EU
representative GPSR@taylorandfrancis.com Taylor & Francis Verlag GmbH,
Kaufingerstraße 24, 80331 München, Germany

Printed and bound by CPI Group (UK) Ltd, Croydon, CR0 4YY
01/05/2025
01858342-0007